Four Scenarios for the Future of the Federal Government:
Collected Essays on Transforming Government

Dr. Bill Brantley

BILL BRANTLEY

Copyright © 2019 Bill Brantley

ISBN-13: 9781091480872

FOUR SCENARIOS OF THE FUTURE OF GOVERNMENT

TABLE OF CONTENTS

Introduction

This book is a collection of essays I wrote for the American Society for Public Administration's online publication, the *PA Times*. I was honored to become a columnist in February 2015 and continue writing my monthly observations on the future of government. It has been a rewarding experience, and I thank the *PA Times* editorial staff for the privilege.

I have made the Washington, D.C. area home twice in my life. The first time was when I came to George Washington University to attend the Graduate School of Political Management. I have been a political campaign wonk since I was recruited to appear in a political campaign event for a grade school friend's father's county prosecutor campaign. I arrived in D.C. at the start of the Republican Revolution in the spring of 1995.

After receiving my Master's in Political Management in the winter of 1996, I applied for the Presidential Management Fellow (then, the Presidential Management Intern program). I thought it would help my political management career to have some experience in working in a government agency. It was during my two years in the PMF program I became fascinated by making government work better.

In 2000, I moved back to my home in Louisville, Kentucky to care for an elderly relative. During that time, I worked for two dot-coms and pursued an MBA (Master of Business Administration) instead of an MPA (Master of Public Administration). I also began part-time teaching at the University of Louisville's Communication Department. After receiving an MBA, I pursued a Ph.D. in Public Administration.

I attended Walden University because it had a program, I could pursue my interests in how the Internet and digital technologies were changing the government. When I was in the political management program, the commercial Internet was affecting political campaigns. I took two independent study classes where I wrote research papers on how the Internet would change political campaigning and the persuasive power of political interest groups. During my time as a

PMF, I watched how federal, state, and local governments adapted to the new world of web sites. In the General Services Administration's Office of Intergovernmental Affairs, I created the first intergovernmental survey of state and local government web sites.

My graduate work at Walden allowed me to research how digital technology was changing the government. I became fascinated by how change succeeds or fails in government. My dissertation was a study on how to best communicate a change vision in a significant local government restructuring.

I came back to D.C. in December of 2008; right in time for the historical change that was the President Obama administration. I worked at the U.S. Office of Personnel Management (OPM) and became an active blogger in the *GovLoop* community. It was a great time to be back in the federal government because of President Obama's emphasis on open data and the open government movement.

During 2011, I was on a one year temporay assignment to OPM's Open Government Project. OPM's Open Government Project differed from the other public agencies because OPM's project focused on the cultural change needed for open data and open government. I also become involved with Drupal4Gov conferences and met many open government enthusiasts.

Between 2012 and 2015, I presented on my agile policy making theories at several academic conferences and wrote a column for the General Services Administration's Digital University and the *PA Times*. At OPM, I worked for the Strategic Workforce Planning Office where I deepened my interest in how federal human resources management would be affected by digital technology.

These essays result from my research and thoughts in how the federal government (and government in general) is changing as digital technologies rapidly evolve. Much has changed since I obtained my first personal computer (a Commodore 64) in the early 80s to my morning ritual of asking Alexa what the weather will be today. You can see the progression as you read the essays which I have kept the same as the time they were published (except for a few grammatical and stylistic changes thanks to the new artificial-intelligence, cloud-based writing assistants).

There are fifty-two essays with fifty being divided up into four sections: Transforming Government, Transforming the Government Workforce, Transforming Government Policy, and Miscellaneous Thoughts on Public Administration. The fifty essays represent the interplay between the challenges of digital technology and its effect on government human resources management and government policy.

I start the book with two of my favorite essays. The first on the four scenarios of the future of the federal government were written during my time in OPM's Open Government detail. I've revisited the four scenarios in the last eight years with a new update, *Gov Trek*, which is the final chapter.

The second essay on artificial intelligence (AI) and blockchain-powered digital autonomous organizations (DAO) represents how radically AI and associated technologies will change governments. It is also my favorite title because of the play on a classic *The Simpsons* line.

Please jump in where you see something interesting. I hope the essays stimulate your thoughts and I would appreciate hearing from you. Being a writer can feel like you are shouting into an empty house and receiving the occasional answer from a reader is very welcome. Even if the reader disagrees with everything I write, the exchange of ideas is the most gratifying part of writing a column.

THE FOUR SCENARIOS OF THE FUTURE OF GOVERNMENT (2011)

"Greetings, my friend. We are all interested in the future, for that is where you and I are going to spend the rest of our lives. And remember, my friend, future events such as these will affect you in the future." (From the opening of *Plan Nine from Outer Space*[i])

The idea for this posting came from a remark by a participant at the OpenGov Summit at NASA[ii]. It was a great event with some powerful ideas for OpenGov and Gov 2.0. I was in a session where we discussed applying social network analysis to knowledge management when one person stated that agencies have to implement Gov 2.0 or it will be forced on them.

A rather provocative statement! I thought about this as I took the afternoon off to wander around the Air and Space Museum. Being a student of scenario planning, I thought of four scenarios where the government takes the lead in Gov 2.0 or misses the Gov 2.0 change. Now the idea behind scenario planning is not to predict the future but to use the scenarios to understand the potentials and challenges of current trends. An excellent example of this is Business 2.0's 2006 scenarios about the future of Google[iii].

First Scenario – SteamGov

This scenario borrows from the steampunk genre[iv] in describing a future where the government attempts to implement Gov 2.0, but the rest of the world has moved on to Web 3.0 or even Web 4.0.

Government IT is still a generation behind the current technology available to citizens thus limiting the engagement offered by the agencies. Large, centralized IT architectures dominate the agencies and employees are continually frustrated by the underpowered workstations they have to deal with especially when their own personal technology is much more powerful. There are small pockets of innovation and pilot projects, but organizational cultures prevent scaling up these innovations to the agency.

Second Scenario – Google.Gov

Following a Supreme Court ruling that narrows the definition of inherently governmental, most government functions are outsourced to the private and nonprofit sectors. A Google-like company consolidates most of the outsourcing contractors into one contracting firm that applies the latest technology and business practices to delivering a diverse range of government services. The Executive Branch now consists of the White House staff and a larger GAO. The new GAO administers the mega contract that governs the quality and accountability of government services provided by the huge contracting firm.

Third Scenario – LabGov

Still suffering under crushing budget constraints and frustrated by the continuing number of programs forced onto the states by the Federal government, state governments see Gov 2.0 as the way out of their fiscal mess. Living up to Justice Brandeis' metaphor as "laboratories of democracy," the state governments experiment with the latest open-source technologies, agile project management, and any other IT or management innovations that promise greater efficiency at lower costs and higher citizen satisfaction.

Citizens respond with enthusiasm and petition to have more federal programs (and funds) transferred to the states because they can manage services better, faster, and cheaper than the federal government. States form into regional and programmatic associations that shift the federal-state balance-of-power from the national government to regional governmental organizations (As an example, see Utah's Laboratory of Democracy Act of 2010[v]).

Fourth Scenario – InnoGov

In 2011 the civilian equivalent of the Defense Advanced Research Projects Administration was established. Its mandate is to be the project management office for Gov 2.0, and the office seeks innovative Gov 2.0 projects, funds the development of these projects, and helps other agencies to copy the innovations. New radical management techniques are introduced, and organizational cultures become more collaborative and innovative.

By 2014 the federal government is the leading innovator in IT and management practices and helps to revitalize the private and non-profit sectors with its technology/best practices transfer programs. Citizen engagement and trust in government rises while the cost-savings and greater efficiencies bring about an era of budget surpluses.

I, FOR ONE, WELCOME OUR NEW CHATBOT BLOCKCHAIN DIGITAL AUTONOMOUS ORGANIZATIONS (2016)

It is at the intersections of fields where you find the most fascinating and innovative concepts. Recently, a conference on "Open Human Resources and the Cognitive Era" explored the use of chatbots and blockchain technologies in human resources. Human Resources (HR) is quietly undergoing a revolution as many HR practitioners are transforming HR by using open source concepts.

It is fascinating to see how cognitive technologies and cloud technologies are changing HR from a transactional and compliance function to an essential strategic organizational asset. Let us examine three innovative technologies that, joined, can reinvent how Federal agencies do their HR work (and work in general).

We have talked about chatbots before on *DigitalGov* [General Services Administration's Digital University platform]. To recap: chatbots use artificial intelligence to reply to questions asked by users using voice or text input. The most famous chatbot is IBM's Watson, which successively competed on "Jeopardy." More recently, a north London council adopted "Amelia" to help citizens

Unlike chatbots, many of you may not have heard of the blockchain technology. But if you have, you may think it is synonymous with the digital currency, bitcoin. Bitcoin is just one implementation of the blockchain. The blockchain is a sophisticated technology, and so, I like to use this non-technical explanation on how it works.

Think about your bank (or credit union). You have an account or accounts at the bank along with many other customers. You trust the bank to keep a record of your transactions, as do the other customers. Questions about the transactions are answered by examining the transaction records maintained by the bank. The bank is essentially a centralized trust authority because it has the one set of records commonly agreed to by the customers. That trust can be damaged or destroyed if the records are falsified or lost due to crime or accident.

In contrast, blockchain works on a distributed trust model. Imagine that you and other bank customers use blockchain to record transactions. That means that every bank customer receives a copy of the transaction ledger, which is secured by some cryptological key to verify that you have a genuine copy. Every time a new transaction occurs, that record is replicated automatically to all of the transaction ledgers.

Therefore, if something happens to the bank's records, the transactions can still be verified by examining a majority of the blockchain ledgers. The bank is no longer needed as transactions can be verified automatically by checking the blockchain ledgers. Caveat: as with all simplified explanations, I am leaving out some details. Here is a more thorough explanation from the United Kingdom Office of Science.

The Digital Autonomous Organization (DAO; sometimes also known as a "decentralized autonomous organization") takes blockchain technology a step further. Instead of just dealing with financial transactions, DAOs use " smart contracts " that rely on blockchains to verify if contractual obligations have been met.

For example, you could set up a smart contract with the local grocery store. On a set schedule, groceries are automatically delivered to your home and, once your home's artificial intelligence sensor network records the successful grocery delivery, the grocer is automatically paid through a blockchain transaction. In an extreme form, the grocery store is a sophisticated artificial intelligence chatbot that has no human managers. The grocery store is a DAO, which uses "if-then" algorithms to manage the acquisition, storage, and delivery of grocery items without human intervention.

Now, imagine if a government agency used DAOs to manage and provide government services. Applying for and receiving government benefits could be handled by DAOs. Or applying for and obtaining a passport. Federal employees would still be needed to step if there are exceptions to the algorithms or smart contracts, but, otherwise, the DAO can interact with the public through the chatbot while performing the identification and authentication through blockchains.

These are still emerging technologies, and there are many issues to be worked out before fully trusting a DAO or blockchain. It is fascinating to see how these technologies can release the HR worker from the routine processing of transactions to become a creative problem solver that brings better value to the organization. Maybe, the lessons learned from the adoption of cognitive technologies in HR could also help better the other business units in Federal agencies.

(Originally published on General Services Administration's Digital University's *The Data Briefing*)

The Transforming Government Essays

THREE KEY CONCEPTS THAT GOVERNMENTS CAN LEARN FROM LEAN STARTUPS (2015)

Lean startup methodology exploded into the business world with the 2011 publication of Eric Ries' *The Lean Startup*. Eric Ries describes lean startup as using "validated learning" to arrive at a viable business model iteratively. The entrepreneur interviews customers to determine their needs develops a hypothesis around a product or service, and then continually tests the hypothesis with customers until a profitable product or service can be put into the marketplace. Lean startup differs from traditional business startup methods in that the customer is involved even in a product or service is created.

The lean startup has led to some other lean concepts such as lean analytics, lean user experience (UX), and lean marketing. Every phase of business operations can benefit from lean concepts. The lean startup has also been applied to the nonprofit sector through such courses as Acumen's *Lean for Social Good*. The former Federal Chief Technology Officer, Todd Park, advocated using lean startup for government programs such as the Consumer Financial Protection Bureau. The U.S. General Services Administration digital services unit, 18F, uses lean startup principles in providing application development for other Federal agencies.

However, even with the popularity of lean startup, not every organization should use lean startup. It is a new methodology and, admittedly, much hype obscures the trendy practices from tested practices. Like older methodologies such as project management or business process management, there is still a good deal of work and testing to develop a lean startup fully into a reliable method that consistently delivers successful results. There are three key concepts that governments can use to improve their delivery of government services: empathy, metrics that matter and being genuinely lean.

Empathy: Deeply Understanding the Citizens' Needs

Lean startup practitioners spend much of their time interviewing prospective customers before even planning the product or service. The goal is to learn what problems bedevil customers and just how severe is the problem. The idea is to find the "migraine" problem for which a customer is very willing to pay for the solution. Lean startup practitioners do not try to sell to the customer during this time. No, the purpose is to understand the customer's problem fully and to generate possible solutions to the problem. The lean startup practitioner then methodically tests the solutions with the customers. The purpose is to arrive at a solution that solves the problem, which customers recognize will solve the problem, and, most important, customers will pay to solve their problem.

Metrics that Matter: Using Data to Validate Learning

Lean startups thrive on data. Every proposed solution is considered an assumption that must be tested with actual customers before being validated. Many lean startup practitioners observe that the essence of the lean startup methodology is applying the scientific method to starting a business. All these experiments generate data that must be analyzed to arrive at the final product or service.

However, the metrics must matter. There are "vanity metrics" that are misleading and can lead the lean startup down the wrong path. For example, website visits may be a vanity metric because even though there are numerous web visitors; only a tiny percentage will pay for the proposed solution. Useful metrics relates directly to the customers' problem and how willing the customers' are to adopt a proposed solution to their problem.

Being Lean: Carve Away Everything That Doesn't Solve the Customers' Problem

The "lean" in lean startup comes from the intense focus on validating and solving the customers' problem. Any business activity that doesn't directly solve the customers' problem or support the team that is building the solution is considered non-essential to the startup and must be trimmed away. Being lean is vital to the startup because the startup is not just a smaller version of the eventual business model.

In the lean startup methodology, the startup is a set of experiments to find a viable business model that can be scaled up. Thus, there are many solutions to test and discard before the final solution can be found. The faster and more cost-effectively the lean startup can run through the experiment phase; the more likely a successful solution will be found.

Lean Startup for Governments

Adopting all of the lean startup practices will not work in government because of the numerous constraints that government faces that do not affect the private sector. Even so, the three concepts of empathy, metrics that matter, and being lean by focusing on the customers' problem are the foundation for a useful version of lean startup methodology for governments.

REDESIGNING GOVERNMENT AGENCIES USING ORGANIZATIONAL HEALTH, ORGANIZATIONAL AGILITY, AND NETWORK HEALTH (2015)

Implementing policy is just as vital to creating the policy. Agencies need the ability to execute effectively and manage the policies. In my research in how government agencies are designed and operated, I have come across three concepts I use in understanding how agencies can successfully execute their missions and policies.

It is well-understood that technological changes and societal changes have created new types of private sector organizations that would not have existed twenty years ago. New challenges such as climate change and terrorism have also created new demands on governments to respond effectively to these challenges.

Government agencies must also evolve to meet new citizen needs and demands. The question is how to help agencies change effectively. Using organizational health, organizational agility, and network health will best the guide to reforming government agencies.

Organizational Health

Organizational health is defined by Keller and Price in their 2011 book, *Beyond Performance*, as "the ability of an organization to align, execute, and renew itself . . . so that it can sustain exceptional performance over time." For government agencies, organizational health is how effectively the people, processes, and technologies are aligned with the agency's strategic goals.

Under the Keller and Price organizational health model, agencies would be measured along three dimensions: internal alignment, quality of execution, and capacity for renewal. Is everyone in the agency working toward the same goals and can they achieve these goals?

Agencies should examine their performance on these nine elements to answer the questions from the preceding paragraph (adapted from Keller and Price):

Direction - a clear sense of where the organization is heading and how it will get there that is meaningful to all employees.

Leadership - the extent to which leaders inspire actions by others.

Culture and Climate - the shared beliefs and quality of interactions within and across organizational units.

Accountability - the extent to which individuals understand what is expected of them, have sufficient authority to carry it out and take responsibility for delivering results.

Coordination and Control - the ability to evaluate organizational performance and risk, and to address issues and opportunities when they arise.

Capabilities - the presence of institutional skills and talent required to execute strategy and create competitive advantage.

Motivation - the presence of enthusiasm that drives employees to put in the extraordinary effort to deliver results.

External Orientation - the quality of engagement with customers, suppliers, partners, and other external stakeholders to drive value.

Innovation and Learning - the quality and flow of new ideas and the organization's ability to adapt and shape itself as needed.

Organizational Agility

Organizational health is necessary but not sufficient. An agency must have organizational agility to maintain organizational health. Federal agencies have a long tradition of organizational structures with firm boundaries (established by organizational charts) and strict internal and external areas of formal authority (statutes, regulations, executive orders, policies, interagency working agreements, etc.).

Increasingly, however, agencies are recognizing that they, too, exist in a complex adaptive system. Agencies' permeable boundaries are affected daily by external factors (i.e., budgets, social media, unexpected crises), which affect how agencies achieve their missions.

Organizational agility has become and will continue to be a requirement for Federal organizations as external environmental factors (e.g., budget fluctuations, changes in public expectations, unforeseen crises) become more complex and unpredictable. This continuous change requires that modern organizations acquire a flexible and responsive approach to managing people, processes, and technology to achieve their missions.

Agencies must now build the capacity to manage change while pursuing optimal performance and mission accomplishment. Managing with agility incorporates being flexible and open to adopting new business processes while adapting an organization's mindset and culture to constant change.

Agencies must enable leaders, managers, and employees to align toward outcomes while continually scanning for projected changes and preparing to adapt to new requirements and expectations.

Network Health

I am still working on the network health concept, but it has similarities to organizational health. In network health, healthy and agile organizations replace people in the people, processes, and technology triad of organizational health. As Innes and Booher write in *Planning with Complexity* (2010), "[a]t its heart, adaptive governance is about harnessing the power of networks – networks that connect people, ideas, and knowledge in changing combinations across organizations and public problems."

No single government agency, no matter how healthy and agile, can work alone in solving many of the broader challenges facing governments today. It will take a network to manage these problems.

The New Government Agency

I do not yet know what the ideal organizational design is for government agencies. Maybe there is an entire group of organizational designs specific to the mission. Agencies might cycle through organizational models based on the challenges the agency faces. Whatever the plan of the agency, the successful agencies will have organizational health, be organizationally agile, and are valuable contributors in a healthy network of agencies and other entities.

CULTURE AND STRATEGY, NOT TECHNOLOGY, DRIVES DIGITAL TRANSFORMATION IN GOVERNMENT (2015)

Peter Drucker observed that "culture eats strategy for breakfast" when explaining why organizational strategies fail or succeed. I was thinking of this quote when I read the 2015 study of digital businesses by MIT's *Sloan Management Review* and Deloitte. Nearly 4,800 business executives, managers, and analysts from 129 countries and 27 industries were surveyed about the challenges of using digital and social technologies in their organizations.

The title of the 2015 research report captures the significant finding of the study: "Strategy, Not Technology, Drives Digital Transformation." The authors make good points about how to build an effective digital strategy to move an organization toward digital maturity.

Digital maturity for an organization is defined as "where digital has transformed processes, talent engagement, and business models." The authors did not find an organization that is fully digital-mature, but they did see a small percentage of organizations that achieved a high level of digital maturity.

The highly mature digital organizations had a "clear and coherent" digital strategy. However, I think that the authors underemphasize the vital role of culture in supporting digital strategy. There are several valuable observations on how culture enabled successful digital strategy that apply to government agencies. In the next five sections, I will describe how the significant findings of the report can support agency efforts to achieve digital maturity.

Focus on transforming the business and not the technology

Technology is necessary but not enough to becoming a digitally mature organization. As the authors found, digitally immature organizations focused too much on individual technologies and thus had purely operational strategies. The digitally mature organizations focused their approach on transforming their business using digital technologies.

It has been my experience that organizations often buy a software application without considering how the software will aid in the transformation. The organization is attracted to the features of the software and then try to shape the change around the software features. Little attention is given to the cultural implications of technology-driven change.

Employee skill development is key to realizing the strategy

As the study authors found, a vital skill is the ability to understand how digital technologies will transform the business. This skill is essential at all levels of the organization. Digitally mature organizations provide more training to help employees develop the skills while most digitally immature organizations lack this training.

Much of the resistance to change stems from people who do not feel they can perform successfully in the newly-transformed organization. Providing skill training will help employees better accept digital transformation.

Being a Digital Leader is the best way to attract and retain talent

This finding encompasses all generations. All generations from Baby Boomers from Millennials want to work in digitally mature organizations. The Digital Leader finding makes sense as digitally immature organizations often frustrate employees with ineffective technology and complex processes. Digitally mature organizations have a more definite understanding of mission and use digital technology effectively to support the mission.

Risk taking is a cultural norm

Risk taking is a common finding in many of the studies examining innovative modern organizations. What is new in this study is the realization that "employees may be just as risk-averse as their managers and will need support to become bolder." Several of the digitally matures companies use gamification to encourage employees to take risks and learn from their failures. Risk taking may be the most difficult cultural shift for government agencies to adopt as learning from failure runs counter to agency employees being accountable to the agency mission (and efficiently managing public funds). Maybe encouraging experimentation and prototyping with immediate and rich feedback can make government risk taking more palatable than calling it "learning from failure."

Digital strategy comes from the top and requires digitally-fluent leaders

An interesting concept from this finding is that leaders need not be technically adept in digital technologies. Instead, the more critical skill understands how digital technologies will change the organization or, digital fluency. The digitally fluent leader effectively communicates through stories which vividly describes how the organization will become digitally mature. Helping employees to see the new organizational future is a vital leadership skill in all change efforts.

Government becoming digitally mature

President Obama's administration is attempting to transform the digital infrastructure of the Federal government. There have been several innovative and well-designed strategies focusing on open government, open data, and enabling policies such as modernizing government record management. However, to realize the promise of a digitally mature Federal government, the culture in agencies must also be transformed to enable the success of President Obama's digital strategy.

SHOULD GOVERNMENT AGENCIES HAVE DUAL "OPERATING SYSTEMS?" (2015)

People demand more innovation from the government, but they also want dependability. As I often heard in meetings, citizens need government services that are as easy to access as buying something from Amazon.com. People are used to receiving quick, personalized service and products at an ever-increasing rate and with more innovation. Government agencies are working hard to provide innovative services in a customer-friendly way. As recent news stories have shown, many government services are still hard to obtain.

The problem is not lack of innovation. Several agencies from the General Services Administration to the Office of Personnel Management to the Department of Health and Human Services have groups that provide highly innovative solutions. Either in an innovation lab or through 18F, there is no lack of ground-breaking ideas for better government services. However, having a great idea is only part of the solution. Implementing innovation into the agency's existing business processes is where most changes fail. According to some authors, it is because of the difference in the innovation "operating system" versus the execution "operating system."

A Startup Connected to a Mature Organization

John Kotter introduced the concept of dual operating systems in his 2014 book, *Accelerate: Building Strategic Agility for a Faster-Moving World*. He describes how organizations start as a network of individuals where communication and innovation flow freely in a flat, highly-connected small organization. As the organization grows, it becomes hierarchical to efficiently deliver products and services. Hierarchical design is necessary so organizations can build and scale up business processes to provide to a broader customer base. Except, in pursuing efficiency, innovation becomes lost.

Kotter suggests that hierarchical organizations build a startup network inside the organization. Employees would periodically cycle to the startup operating system to develop new services. Then, employees would come back to their jobs in the hierarchical operating system to help integrate the innovations into the hierarchy's business processes. The advantage is that the handoff between the operating systems is a smooth transition for innovation.

Running the Performance Engine While Rebuilding It

Kotter was not the first to suggest the dual operating system. Vjay Govindarajan and Chris Trimble discussed dual operating systems in their 2005 book, *Ten Rules for Strategic Innovators.* They later expanded on the dual operating systems concept in the 2010 book, *The Other Side of Innovation: Solving the Execution Challenge,* by describing how to use an *Innovation Team* to perform innovation experiments. The successful tests are then carefully integrated into the organization's *Performance Engine* (the collection of business processes that handle delivering the organization's services and products). Again, the key lessons are how to conduct the transfer of the innovation from one operating system to the other without severe disruption to the organization's delivery of services.

Staying Out of the Garbage Can

Eventually, adding new business processes while retiring the old business processes will cause an entirely new Performance Engine. This risk building an unfocused and inefficient Performance Engine that is a collection of contradictory business processes. The collection of contradictory business processes is Cohen, March, and Olsen's Garbage Can Model embodied as the organization's new Performance Engine[vi]. How does the government agency plan the implementation of their innovations, so the Performance Engine evolves to deliver the strategic mission better?

As I have written in a previous column ("THREE KEY CONCEPTS THAT GOVERNMENTS CAN LEARN FROM LEAN STARTUPS (2015)"), government agencies can use three techniques from lean startups to help tune their performance engine. The first technique is to focus continually on the customers' needs while also aligning all business processes to the agency's mission. The second technique is to build metrics into the processes to track the performance of the business processes and how well the business processes align with the agency's mission. Relentlessly focusing on carving away processes that don't focus on the customer and the agency's mission is the third lean startup technique. These techniques should guide both operating systems as they collectively build and implement innovations.

Why Government Agencies Need Dual Operating Systems

Government agencies are under enormous pressure to be more innovative in delivering government services while dealing with smaller budgets and fewer resources. Agencies are and have always established dedicated teams to innovation. But as the garbage can model demonstrates, agencies can do a better job of implementing changes into their business processes. Many agencies already have dual operating systems. Realizing the existence of dual operating systems can help agencies improve how innovations are handled between the two operating systems. Dual operating systems, when coordinated effectively, can generate great changes and implement those innovations for better government services.

RETHINKING STRATEGY FOR PUBLIC AGENCIES (2015)

Modern business strategic thinking could be said to have begun in the 1960s. It began when Michael Porter published his thoughts on competition and when three prominent strategic consulting firms (Boston Consulting Group; Bain & Company; and McKinsey & Company) offered strategy formulation services. Strategy consulting is a multibillion-dollar industry with many models and implementations to help organizations set strategic goals, streamline operations, and handle organizational change. Thanks to innovations such as six-sigma and lean manufacturing, many American corporations have experienced tremendous growth and profitability in the last fifty years.

During this same period, trust in the U.S. Federal government, state governments, and local governments declined. Citizens perceived declining quality in government services while their tax burden was increasing. High-profile government reform efforts that borrowed from strategic corporate initiatives were launched by Presidential administrations in the 1970s through to today. If it worked for business, then it should work for the government.

Unfortunately, directly transferring private sector strategies to the public sector have met with mixed results. The mixed results are because private sector strategies work in a different environment from the public sector. Private sector organizations exist to compete in a market by gaining a competitive advantage over its rivals. Making a profit and maximizing shareholders' returns are the driving force behind most corporate strategies. Private sector organizations that are unsuccessful quickly close and disappear from the marketplace.

In contrast, public sector organizations are driven by "public value." As described by Lusk and Birks (2014) in Rethinking Public Strategy, "public value is the value that government co-creates with its citizens and citizens value" (p. 50). Mark Moore of the Harvard University's Kennedy School of Government visualizes public value as consisting of three components. First, there is the "Mandate" or the authorizing or legitimating environment of the public agency. Second, there is the operational capability and capacity of the public agency. Third, there are the "Social Mission" or public value outcomes. Public value fits in well with Lusk and Birk's conception of public strategy as a process to create a strategic intent for a policy then delivered by a public agency.

Lusk and Birks' (2014) view of public strategy as more than merely solving problems and serving customers. As they argue, the problem-solving perspective can narrow the public servants' understanding of a complex issue and create short-term optimal solutions with undesired long-term effects. Also, treating citizens as customers are not always appropriate in all public service contexts. Is the job seeker is the customer of the state employment agency? On the surface, maybe. However, Lusk and Birks assert that the job seeker is a co-producer of value. The employment agency can help the job seeker find a job but, the job seeker must show up on time for interviews, dress appropriately, and participate in training designed to help him or her increase their chances of finding work.

Therefore, if governments are more than just problem solvers and citizens are more than only customers, what is the role of government? Lusk and Birks' (2014) advocate governments as shapers of the future. The world faces many significant challenges: climate change, terrorism, resource shortages, etc. Corporations may tackle these issues, but that is not their fundamental purpose. Many non-profits also exist to take on these challenges. However, their resources are constrained, and their authority is limited. The government is the only entity large enough and with authority – given by their citizens – to tackle these problems and shape the future toward better outcomes.

What is needed to develop a model of strategic thinking for the public sector? First, realize the barriers that prevent public agencies from thinking of the future. Because of shrinking resources and increasing demands for public services, agencies are forced into short-term thinking. There are often few resources to build for future capabilities or even to meet current needs. Agencies often muddle through with what they have. When agencies do think about the future, they see it through the "lens of now" in which policymakers assume a linear progression of current trends. Policy makers also fail to think clearly of the future due to groupthink and expert bias. Breaking free of these barriers is the first step in public strategic thinking.

The second step in public strategic thinking is to examine and understand the drivers of change. The drivers of change are often demographic, technology, economic, and societal. These are extensive categories, and thus, trend analysis can help spot the most influential trends. When doing trend analysis, be wary of just extrapolating trends linearly. Change is often disruptive and what appears to be an insignificant blip today could be a significant benefit or challenge.

The third step is to realize that predicting a future is futile. However, envisioning several futures is not. Use scenarios to describe several futures to reach. Shaping the future is the best way for governments to help create public value.

AN INTERVIEW WITH WILLIAM EGGERS ON DIGITALLY TRANSFORMING GOVERNMENT (2016)

Interview with noted public administration scholar, William Eggers, whose book, *Delivering on Digital: A Guide to Government Transformation*, will be released in June 2016.

Why the topic of Government and Digital?

In a world where any song can be played instantly, any product on Earth can arrive at your doorstep in 24 hours, and a ride is never more than three minutes away from your phone, it's inconceivable to have the patience of waiting weeks or months when waiting for a product or service.

The bar has been raised so high, and we have become spoiled in our assumptions so suddenly and intensely, that for anything to operate less fast, intuitively, or efficient than Amazon, Google, Uber, Facebook, Netflix, or Airbnb, then it's an instant death knell that few companies can escape.

Government cannot be immune to this massive change. In a constantly changing, evolving, adapting digital world, some parts of government are still living back in the 90s. This is unacceptable.

But there is hope, lots of hope and it's because of both the hope and the necessity that I wrote this book.

What is the digital infrastructure like in most government agencies today?

Call it the "green screen" syndrome. Many government entities continue to handle critical public business processes on computers that today's IT elite probably wouldn't even recognize; large piles of plastic, steel and wire that take up a lot of room and operate in the most unwieldy fashion... with a green screen interface. It's a world of COBOL systems built decades ago, pre-World Wide Web.

They are "legacy systems," and they have risen to the top of the list of operational concerns when it comes to streamlining and securing how government work gets done today. In a rapidly evolving era of "apps" and "Clouds," legacy systems continue to underpin an alarming percentage of the operational and data storage work that government – at all levels – actually does.

What's the biggest challenge that government faces on its path to digital transformation?

Challenges to digital transformation abound: 30-year old legacy computer systems, slow-moving procurement systems, and lack of digital skills in the workforce, to name a few. But the biggest obstacle is culture. The digital mindset puts a premium on openness, experimentation, and fast failure in order to learn more quickly.

Such a mindset is often at odds with government cultures rooted in rules, regulations, and mores that have evolved over decades or even centuries. Whereas a key tenet of digital delivery holds that you don't know the right approach for users before you test it, the public sector's requirement-driven culture, often based on legislation, assumes policymakers have all the answers a priori. The bottom line: there's little reward in the public sector for taking risks, and developing digital government can be risky business.

What is a "digital mindset" and how is it different from the mindset that most public sector organizations have?

A digital mindset is simply different from the attitudes driving most organizations, especially in the public sector. It's a different way of thinking about customers; a different way of launching products and services; a different way of working.

Five characteristics tend to be common among individuals and organizations that understand the opportunities inherent in digital transformation: a belief in openness, user-centricity, co-creation, simplicity and agility. In many respects, the digital worldview is as important to the future of government as the labels "conservative" or "liberal" were to its past.

According to the Pew Research Center, trust in government is at historically low levels as only 19% of Americans trust the Federal government to do what is right. With American citizens this distrustful and skeptical of government's ability, what can policymakers do to convince the American public to support the digital transformation of the Federal government?

One attitude has driven excellence at Uber, Airbnb, Amazon, Netflix, and Apple in the last five years. They start with dedication to the user. It's the user who pays their bills and so if the user is not happy, or in any way slowed down or frustrated by the technology, then the whole business crumbles. So they design simple and intuitive experiences.

Government services can no longer be rigid. Digital solutions allow us to adapt services to the user. This in turn will enhance trust in government.

The old mindset and lack of user focus can have an unintended negative consequence: loss of trust in government. As Mike Bracken, the founder of UK's Government Digital Service, points out, "When people stop believing in government, they stop believing in some quite fundamental things about how society works, like paying tax for the good of everyone or obeying the rules of society—these are the natural consequences of government losing the trust of its users."

THREE AGILE PROJECT MANAGEMENT METHODS GOVERNMENT AGENCIES CAN IMPLEMENT NOW (2016)

The headline sounds like clickbait, but there are incremental steps that agencies can take in creating an agile project management culture. As more agencies realize the limitations of traditional project management, some offices are using agile project management methods to deliver projects successfully. Agile project management has been widely accepted in many government IT offices. Other agency offices, such as procurement or facilities, have also adopted agile project management.

Adopting agile project management requires cultural change. The acceptance of incrementally solving a steady stream of iterations heavily based on regular customer feedback. This cultural change is why some agile practitioners will argue that implementing agile management requires establishing the agile management practices together.

The all-or-nothing agile management advocates have a point. There are examples of unsuccessful attempts to combine agile project management methods with traditional project management methods. However, there seem just as many examples of successfully combining agile project management and traditional project management. In my particular case of bringing project management to Federal HR and training, I use three essential agile tools to supplement traditional project management methods. These tools are easy to explain, easy to implement, and can help prepare the culture for implementing agile project management.

User Stories

User stories are how agile practitioners gather requirements for an application or project product. It's as easy to implement as having a stack of note cards and collecting the project customers into a meeting room. Then, the customers tell the project manager what features they want in the final product. The customers phrase their requests in this structure: "As a [role], I want a/an [something] so that I can [realize a benefit]." For example, "as a training facilitator, I want a registration list sorted by job role so that I can group participants into the appropriate training groups."

The advantage of user stories is that it is an effective way to collect and organize the many feature requests that customers will have. Doing user stories in a collaborative setting also helps customers merge duplicate features and determine what features are necessary versus features nice to have.

Feature Triangle

Once the project manager has a stack of user stories, the next step is to categorize the user stories into features that are the most necessary to the least essential. In traditional project management, there are the "Triple Constraints" which is often depicted as a triangle. One side of the triangle is the budget, the second side is time, and the third side is scope (the features expected of the project product). The triangle illustrates the constraints that project managers must balance to complete the project. Usually, one constraint must be sacrificed to achieve the other two constraints. Often that means the project is delivered late, over the budget, or without all of the desired features. Usually, the project product is of no value to the customers.

In the feature triangle, it is assumed there will not be enough time and money for all features. The idea is to start with the most-needed feature first, then the second most-needed feature, and so on. That way, if the project budget is cut or the needs to be stopped early, the customers still have value from the project product completed to that point.

Information Radiators

The other name for information radiators better defines their purpose: big visual charts. Agile project management has information radiators that describe what tasks must be done, what tasks have been completed, expected completion dates, and other project status information. The charts are easily understood by the project team, customers, and stakeholders.

A central information radiator is a Kanban chart. In its simplest form, a Kanban chart has three columns with these headings: "To Be

Done," "Doing," and "Done." Tasks are placed into one of the three columns depending on whether the task is waiting to be worked on, is being worked on, or is completed. A similar information radiator, the burndown chart, shows how much work is to be done versus the time left.

Why Start with These Three Tools?

A project creates something within a set amount of time and within a budget. Whether it is a traditional project or agile project, tasks are the heart of the project. These three tools determine what tasks are needed, in what order of priority, and how the project is doing overall. Whether it is an information technology project or policy project, these three tools can help deliver a great product.

NOW IS THE TIME TO REINVENT LEGACY GOVERNMENT PROCESSES (2016)

A University of Maryland colleague likes to tell this story about his previous career as a Federal government employee. Back in the 1970s, he worked at the newly formed Department of Energy. He is an architect and was hired to help create the standards for energy-efficient buildings. In his work, my colleague had to procure building materials, appliances, and testing equipment. After experiencing some frustration with the Federal procurement process, he mapped out the entire procurement process to understand where the bottlenecks were.

He sketched out the process on a roll of newsprint. When he finished and verified the process, he scheduled a meeting with his boss. When the boss came into the meeting room, my colleague had the newsprint taped to the wall. The newsprint covered all four walls as it circled the meeting room. The boss, having realized the problem, worked with my colleague to streamline the procurement process down to fifteen steps while still maintaining the accountability and fairness of the procurement process.

I tell this story to illustrate the point that the real focus on dealing with legacy IT systems in the Federal, state, and local governments should not just be on the IT systems themselves. The focus should also be on the legacy processes that the legacy IT systems support.

The Government Accountability Office (GAO) May 25, 2016, report found that 75% of the $80 billion spent on Federal government IT went to operating and maintaining legacy systems[vii]. For example, large mainframe COBOL systems that handle the personnel information and payrolls for the Federal government workforce or the 8-inch floppy disks that control America's nuclear arsenal. There have been calls from the White House and the Congress to modernize these systems. However, the calls seem to recommend replicating the systems from the legacy mainframes to a cloud solution. There does not seem much consideration given to re-engineering the processes first to determine if the process is still needed and then, streamlining the process while taking advantage of the new capabilities offered by the new digital technologies.

There are new methods and technologies for re-engineering processes that can help modernize government processes both internal and external. We can also look to examples such as Estonia that have an amazingly efficient and effective digital government infrastructure. In the sections below, I describe four methods and technologies that can overhaul current Federal, state, and local government processes.

Process Mining

Process mining is a relatively new analytical technique born out of big data analytics. Using an event log that records how information and transactions flow between steps in a process, a process miner can map the actual processes in a system. Process mapping is similar to my colleague's mapping of the procurement process on newsprint but with more detailed data and the ability to map processes in real time.

Adaptive Case Management

Another method used successfully in re-engineering government processes is adaptive case management (ACM). ACM starts with a simple process supported by collaborative tools. As workers deal with cases, the lessons they learn from each unique case are captured and used to refine the process. ACM's advantages over traditional business process management are that ACM processes evolve upward based on real experiences with cases rather than being a top-down imposed process created based on assumptions about ideal cases.

Chatbots

Chatbots have been around since the 1970s but, thanks to advances in artificial intelligence, voice processing, and deep learning, chatbots have become more responsive and sophisticated. The best example is IBM's Watson, which won on Jeopardy and is now being used in a variety of medical and business applications. The primary advantage of chatbots is that they provide a friendly and intuitive interface that hides the complexity of a process. Therefore, instead of a citizen having to navigate several screens of forms to request a government service, the citizen can use a chatbot to hold an interactive conversation to more easily apply for and receive a government service.

Blockchain

Blockchain technology uses a distributed trust model to manage and verify transactions. Blockchain supported the Bitcoin currency and is now being used to handle transactions such as registering copyrights, recording academic credentials, and verifying identities. The advantages of blockchain technology are that users control their information and transactions; no need for a third party to ensure trust; and all transactions are transparent, faster, and cost less.

The government has an excellent opportunity to increase citizen engagement and citizen satisfaction by taking advantage of the new digital technologies and new process management methods. Citizens are used to great digital experiences thanks to Amazon.com, Facebook, and Google. Other governments such as the United Kingdom and Estonia have used digital technology to re-engineer their processes. The Federal, state, and local governments are taking the critical step in overhauling their IT infrastructures. Now is the best time to take advantage of new technologies and methods to reinvent government processes.

WHY GOVERNMENT NEEDS MORE ENTERPRISE-FOCUSED MOBILE APPS (2016)

According to a report from the IBM Center for the Business of Government, the U.S. federal government has released nearly 300 mobile apps for citizens. These apps range from general informational services to crowdsourcing projects to providing government services. Federal agencies have been doing well in fulfilling the 2012 Digital Government Strategy's mandate of providing "high-quality digital government information and services . . . anywhere, anytime, on any device" (from the IBM Report).

However, the federal government has not taken advantage of the enterprise-focused (EF) mobile app revolution. EF mobile apps help employees by providing organizational information services or support employee collaboration. The private sector has rapidly adopted numerous EF mobile apps for data analytics, human resources processes and supporting distributed teams. There are maybe 20 EF mobile apps among five federal government agencies and, as the IBM Report indicates, there seem few prospects for building more federal EF mobile apps.

Not created more EF apps is a missed opportunity. The federal government can directly benefit from the increased productivity and collaboration brought about by building more EF mobile apps. Indirectly, the government can benefit through increased internal agency collaboration while developing and implementing information technology (IT) solutions more rapidly and effectively. Federal agencies can realize these benefits by taking these three steps.

Break Down the Organizational Silos

Before building more federal EF mobile apps, government agencies will need to re-examine their existing business processes. There are numerous examples of failed government projects where agencies tried to automate existing manual processes that proved too cumbersome or unadaptable to automation. As the private sector has learned, EF mobile apps force the organization to break down silos. Silos prevent the knowledge flow and collaboration that the processes supporting EF mobile apps need to work effectively. Before designing an EF mobile app, organizations first need to redesign their processes.

Use Human-Centered Design (HCD) for EF Government Apps

The same methods that designed the existing business processes cannot be used for developing the new EF mobile apps processes. Listing requirements, going away to build an app without further input and then presenting the app as a fait accompli is the formula for making an EF mobile app that will not be used by employees. Instead, use HCD to learn the needs of the EF mobile app users fully. Build prototypes to continually test the effectiveness of the app while ensuring users will enthusiastically accept it.

Standardize EF Mobile App Development with Design Patterns, Components, Modules, and DevOps

Agile development, coupled with HCD, can help agencies overcome the barriers that limit EF mobile app development. Federal agencies suffer from declining IT budgets, legacy systems, lack of mobile app development talent and ambiguity around the agencies' strategic goals. Components and modules can help standardize EF mobile app development while rapidly increasing app development and implementation using shared design patterns.

Design patterns are repeatable templates that guide the overall design and functionality of mobile apps. Components are shared pieces of codes that provide user interface elements for an app (such as a submit button or a calendar select box). Modules are like components but offer more features that can help the app connect to data sources or present a data graph. There are enough common internal business processes in federal agencies they can pool together resources to create standard governmentwide EF mobile apps.

Federal agencies can also benefit from adopting DevOps in not only developing EF mobile apps but also in developing and deploying all agency IT products and services. DevOps encourages better communication between developers and the other IT professionals who implement the developer's solutions. DevOps also establishes a process of more rapidly building, testing and deploying software while increasing the reliability of software. The same emphasis on collaboration among the IT units can also be spread to the other groups in the agency.

Conclusion

The federal government has proved it can build useful and well-designed mobile apps for citizens. Just examine the listings on the Federal Government Mobile Apps Directory to see the full range of apps from almost every one of the federal agencies. Mobile apps for citizens have an immediate payoff for the federal government. Federal agencies can attain more substantial, long-term benefits by devoting time and resources to building cross-government EF mobile apps using a shared governmentwide library of design patterns, components, and modules. Building EF mobile apps compel the agencies to modernize their business processes, break down organizational silos, increase collaboration and use HCD and DevOps to build better IT applications more effectively.

FOUR QUESTIONS TO ASK BEFORE DIGITALLY TRANSFORMING THE GOVERNMENT AGENCY (2017)

Most organizations are digitally transforming themselves or at least planning to convert digitally. With the advent of cloud computing, application programming interfaces (APIs), big data, and artificial intelligence, organizations are under pressure to transform for various reasons digitally. One reason is to become more competitive in the marketplace while another closely-related reason is to provide better services for their customers. Other causes include better employee engagement, cost-savings, and the prestige of being a cutting-edge organization.

Public sector organizations are also under pressure to digitally transform beginning with the 1995 advent of the commercial Internet. Many government services are available online, and government data sets are being publicly released daily. National governments such as Estonia have fundamentally transformed how their government operates. Both the United States and the United Kingdom have established digital services teams to lead digital transformation efforts.

In a recent *MIT Sloan Management Review* (Spring 2017) article by Stephen J. Andriole, he writes that digital transformation is more than just upgrading software or improving a process. Digital transformation is "a planned digital shock to what may be a reasonably functioning system." Because of the fundamental changes that digital transformation brings, government agencies should think carefully before undertaking the digital transformation journey. These four questions were adopted from Mr. Andriole's article.

Question One: Does the Agency Understand Its Processes?

Before digitally transforming a process or processes, the agency should determine how well it understands its existing operations. In my personal experience, agencies have documented standard operating procedures (SOP) for their methods. However, when I have compared the SOPs to the actual processes, I have found significant variations. The differences may be because of new requirements, changes in personnel, changes in policy, and so on. Thus, before digitally transforming a process, the agency should confirm that the process – as it is practiced – is understood.

Question Two: Is Your Agency Successful with Its Existing Processes?

Once the agency thoroughly understands its current processes, the next question is to ask if the process or processes should be digitally transformed. If the existing process is working well regarding delivering the government service(s) and the citizens are satisfied with the process, then carefully consider how the digital transformation will improve the process. Will it be a significant improvement such as increasing the ease of obtaining the service(s) or it will be much cheaper for the agency to support the process? Is the perceived benefit (both from the agency perspective and the stakeholders' perspective) worth the disruption to the existing process for the new digital process? It is the rare digital transformation project that goes as planned, so the pain of moving to a new process will be higher than anticipated. Unless the new process(es) are less than 10X better, the digital transformation project is not worth the effort.

Question Three: Is the Agency Using Its Existing Digital Technology Assets?

Government agencies spend a great deal of money on information technology. A large proportion of that spending goes to maintaining legacy systems, but there are investments in new technologies. Again, from personal observations, I have seen agencies purchase technologies not fully utilized. For example, at one agency I worked for, there was a document routing system. The purpose of the document routing system was to automate the routing and collection of signatures for policy documents. I was on a task force to determine how to upgrade the document routing system with a new software application. I proposed using the existing Outlook mail system and add a relatively inexpensive electronic signature module to serve as the replacement document routing system. Unfortunately, my suggestion was rejected for an expensive piece of software. This experience did teach me about the unrealized potential in many agency's existing digital technology assets.

Question Four: Do the Agency's Executives Support the Digital Transformation?

This question is the most important. If the senior management does not support the digital transformation project, the project will fail. Digital transformation projects are especially risky for senior managers because the odds of a change project succeeding hovers around 30% to 35%. Digital transformation projects are high-visibility, often expensive, and resource-intensive. Failed digital transformation projects are career-killers for the executive sponsor. There has to be a compelling business case, and a high probability of success before senior management feel comfortable in supporting the digital transformation project.

Digital transformation projects have great potential for improving government. However, digital transformation projects have a high chance of failing. Agencies should consider carefully if the benefits outweigh the risks of digitally transforming agency processes.

COMPLEXITY ECONOMICS AND GOVERNMENT INNOVATION (2017)

The federal government, through the General Services Administration (GSA), is piloting projects involving innovative technologies. There are pilots for artificial intelligence applications, chatbots, and blockchains. About thirty federal agencies are working with GSA to determine how to use emerging digital technologies to deliver government services to citizens. It is the second round of technological innovation I have seen in my career as a federal employee. As in the first round of technological innovation, there is an over-emphasis on the "cool factor" of the new technologies and an under-emphasis on re-inventing agency business processes to support the latest digital technologies.

The Federal Government Meets the World-Wide Web

I started my federal career in the summer of 1997 as a Presidential Management Fellow (then, the title was "Presidential Management Intern"). I began work at the Social Security Administration (SSA) in the Earnings and Enumeration Branch. The Earnings and Enumeration Branch provided management analysis on the assigning and use of Social Security numbers. We were experimenting with web sites and technologies like Microsoft's Active Server Pages to produce interactive web pages.

After nine months at SSA, I rotated to the Office of Intergovernmental Affairs in the General Services Administration. I was fortunate to be assigned as support to the Clinton Administration's Reinventing Government web site projects. I helped conduct one of the first surveys of how the federal, tribal, state, and local governments used the emerging web technologies to provide public-facing government services. There were many impressive pilot projects, and the highlight of my Presidential Management Fellowship was an online database of innovative government web sites I created for the intergovernmental community.

I left the federal government in 1999 and did not return until 2008. Between 2000 and 2009, I pursued both an MBA in project management and a Ph.D. in Public Policy and Management. In my studies, I watched Web 1.0 become Web 2.0 and how governments worldwide adopted new digital technologies. During these nine years, I read and wrote about the theories and methods for building digital organizations. I continue to study and write about digital transformation as more are being discovered each day. However, there is one early influential work I continually turn to understand how organizations can effectively transform digitally.

Beinhocker's Theory of Economic Evolution: Physical Technologies, Social Technologies, and Business Plans

In 2006, I read Eric D. Beinhocker's *The Origin of Wealth: Evolution, Complexity, and the Radical Remaking of Economics*. Dr. Beinhocker does a masterful job of re-making economic theory into a dynamic, evolving system in which innovation and knowledge build wealth. The centerpiece of his argument is how economic evolution works. Economic units called "Business Plans" (BP) compete in the market against each other to produce profits that allow BPs to survive and thrive. BPs comprise two types of technologies. The first type is "Physical Technologies" which are defined by Beinhocker as "methods and designs for transforming matter, energy, and information from one state into another in pursuit of goal or goals" (p. 244). The second type is "Social Technologies" which are "methods and designs for organizing people in pursuit of a goal or goals" (p. 262).

According to Dr. Beinhocker, successful BPs have the right mix of physical technologies and social technologies that work together to effectively and efficiently execute the strategies and processes of the BP. The purpose of economic evolution is for BPs to continually refine the mix of technologies as the BPs interact with other BPs in the market.

Government Innovation as Influenced by Economic Evolution

Dr. Beinhocker's economic evolution can also be applied to government innovation even though government projects are not market-driven. With government projects and programs, the goal is to effectively deliver government services with the most efficient use of federal funds. A government project/program BP with the optimum blend of physical technologies and social technologies will, theoretically, receive more citizen support and public funding than less-optimal government project/program BPs. The key is the mix of physical technologies and social technologies.

Finding the optimum mix of social technologies with physical technologies is what I see missing in the federal government pilot projects involving the new digital technologies. For example, consider the implications for new social technologies inherent in implementing the physical technology of blockchains. A recent Gartner analysis suggests that **early blockchain success will be limited.** It is not a problem with physical technology. Instead, it is an issue with developing the appropriate social technologies around implementing and using blockchains. "**The researchers [Joh-David Lovelock and David Furlonger] believe the technological challenges of blockchain are solvable in the near term. Radical changes in business processes and operational norms will take a longer time to manifest in a company or ecosystem, they said.**"[viii]

It took time for agencies to change their business processes to use the technologies of Web 1.0 and Web 2.0. Perhaps some departments in the agencies are still working out how to use Web 2.0 effectively. The new digital technologies projects can have more impact if there is equal attention paid to social technologies and physical technologies.

THE VALUE OF FEDERAL GOVERNMENT DATA IN TRANSFORMING GOVERNMENT AGENCIES (2017)

The U.S. federal government is probably one of the biggest producers (if not the biggest) producer of data. Every day, thousands of federal workers collect, create, analyze, and distribute massive amounts of data from weather forecasts to economic indicators to health statistics. Federal government data is a significant driver of the American economy as businesses use the data to decide or blend the government data into products and services sold to consumers.

Just how valuable is federal government data? How is the value of information measured? A **recent book** attempts to develop a framework to monetize, manage, and measure data as an organizational asset. *Infonomics* is the framework for helping organizations best value and manage their data assets. Although infonomics is intended for private sector organizations, I can see many applications for federal agencies.

Measuring the Value of Data

Probably the most valuable infonomics concepts are the *Information Performance Gap* (IPG) and the *Information Vision Gap* (IVP). The IPG is the "difference between the realized value of the information asset and its probable value." Closely related is the IVP which is the "difference between the probable and potential information valuations." These concepts are valuable to federal agencies because it gives a new perspective on federal data. As agencies work with their data, are the agencies realizing the value of government information? With the emerging techniques of infonomics, agencies can better measure the value of their information.

Using Data to Transform Government Agencies

Accurately measuring the value of federal data will aid agencies in digitally transforming. Accurately measuring federal data value is one process for changing government agencies that heavily relies on data assets:

Locating and preparing the data assets - Locating and preparing data assets is the hard work of creating a data-driven organization. Consider the vast number of data sources in the average Federal agency. Where the data is located, how is it stored, what types of technology are needed to access and manipulate the data, and how to extract the data. Agency data sources haphazardly grow which means there is a multitude of technologies that silo the data sources from each other. As I have found in gaining my data science certification, much of the data scientist's work is locating and cleaning the data to prepare it for analysis. Determining and preparing data assets can be the costliest and time-intensive task in creating the data-driven organization.

Establishing data partnerships - It is a rare organization where all the data resides in one office or department. Often, data sources are spread throughout the organization and subject to different departmental jurisdictions. Delicate negotiations must create data sharing partnerships and enterprise-wide information governance. Data partnerships may also require going outside the organization to establish access to vital data sources. Creating and managing data partnerships will also take much time and can easily be derailed by even one or two dissenters.

Leadership views data as a strategic asset - Once the hard work of steps one and two are accomplished, being a data-driven organization requires ongoing senior leadership support. Senior leaders must champion the use of analytics to inform agency decisions and support the results of data analysis even if the analysis runs counter to the leadership's initial assumptions. Senior leaders also must promote the governance of data assets and maintaining data partnerships.

Using data for organizational innovation - However, using data assets to create organizational innovations for the agencies is a promising area. Using analytics can help agencies redesign offices to take better advantage of existing agency talent to meet new strategic mission requirements. Analytics can also help agencies to develop new citizen services to meet public demand more effectively.

Using IPG and IVP to measure federal agency information will help senior leadership best extract the value of the data for organizational innovation. Infonomic measurement techniques will give a monetary value to federal information which will aid senior leaders in making return-on-investment and budgetary decisions about the data.

Mapping Data Ecosystems

Another useful application of infonomics is using it in mapping data ecosystems. In a column for General Services Administration' DigitalGov, I described a project by the Congressional Research Service to **map the big data ecosystem of agriculture.** The mapping project gave a "**high-level overview of how big data flows in the agriculture ecosystem.**" Using the infonomic measures, we can also more accurately track how value is created and distributed in large data ecosystems.

Federal government data plays a significant role in the American economy, but this role has been obscured because it is difficult to measure the value of information. With the emergence of infonomics, we have methods for better measuring and managing the value of information. Once citizens can see the monetary impact of Federal government data, citizens and businesses will help in closing the information performance gap to realize the value of Federal government data.

USING ADAPTIVE SPACES TO INCREASE INNOVATION IN GOVERNMENT AGENCIES (2018)

"People will always resist change" is an oft-quoted truism by both management practitioners and academics. Because most change agents believe that people in organizations will resist change, the change agents use two tactics for organizational change. The first is to convince people that their attitudes about change are wrong so they will willingly accept the change. The other is to overwhelm the resistance with the need for change so they will go along with the change. However, what if the belief that people resist change is not entirely accurate?

According to Dr. Steven Kelman, the view that people resist change is "often oversimplified and misleading, and that common change strategies growing out of this view are therefore incomplete as well" (from *Unleashing Change: A Study of Organizational Renewal in Government*, 2005). Kelman's research demonstrates there is often a group of organizational members – the "Change Vanguard" – that are waiting for organizational change because of their dissatisfaction with the status quo. Activating the change vanguard is one tactic of initiating organizational change. The second Kelman tactic helps consolidate change by having the change feed on itself. Change feeding on itself is the use of positive feedback and time to increase the number of people who support organizational change.

Kelman used these tactics in his efforts for procurement reform during his time as a senior procurement policy official at the Office of Management and Budget between 1993 and 1997. The federal government is undergoing another period of procurement reform spurred by the adoption of agile project management by many of the government agencies. From my observations as a federal government employee and agile project management practitioner, there is a change vanguard as evidenced by the 400 plus members of the government agile project management community, the U.S. Digital Service, and the General Services Administration's Technology Transformation Services. However, it may be too early to determine if the change is feeding on itself. There are still significant organizational barriers to the new procurement reform and the adoption of agile project management.

How Organizations Resist Change

There is an "inherent tension between organizing and innovating" (Kelman, 2005). It takes a lot of resources and effort to create a high-functioning organization. Organizations need to "develop structures, training, a culture, and incentives to enable them to do their current job well" as Kelman writes. Organizations recruit people that fit the current organizational processes and rewards organizational members for adhering to the current organization's culture. Existing power relationships also discourages change. Still, the biggest barrier to change may be the organization's shared mental models that essentially blind the organization and its members to the need for change. In bureaucratic organizations, change is even harder because rules and policies "limit the competence of employees and thus their capacity to behave differently," according to Kelman.

How Adaptive Spaces Could Overcome Organizational Resistance to Change

Dr. Michael Arena, the Chief Talent Officer of the General Motors Corporation, recently published *Adaptive Space* (2018). In his book, Arena describes private sector companies are using the concept of "adaptive space" to overcome the built-in barriers to change in organizations. He describes adaptive space as "the free trade zone for ideas within large complex organizations." Adaptive spaces allow for connections and interactions between "people, ideas, information, and resources" in new and innovative ways. Adaptive spaces provide a "social bridge to transport ideas from entrepreneurial pockets found throughout the organization into the more formal operational system."

Key to the success of adaptive spaces are the "4D Connections:" Discovery Connections, Development Connections, Diffusion Connections, and Disruption Connections.

Discovery Connections: These connections are made by "brokers" who create links between groups and individuals. Brokers help the flow of ideas by overcoming the organizational silos to open up access from the entrepreneurial pockets to other entrepreneurial pockets and the larger organization.

Development Connections: Connectors create entrepreneurial pockets and help the pockets to refine and scale their ideas. Connectors work best by developing the social cohesion between the members of entrepreneurial pockets.

Diffusion Connections: Energizers create positive energy in the organizational networks. "Energizers tap into existing relationships, spark the interests of others, and unleash the passion necessary for learning, insights, and adaptation." They create the conditions for the innovations to diffuse through the organization.

Disruptive Connections: Challengers are the final step in bringing about organizational change from the adaptive space. Challengers "leverage the discovery connections of brokers, the development interactions of connectors, and the diffusion connection of energizers to provoke disruption. Challengers, therefore, open up Adaptive Space to create a new normal."

Adaptive Spaces for Government

There are many entrepreneurial pockets of innovation in local, state, and federal governments. What may help government agencies to become more agile and innovative is recognizing the change vanguard and appreciating the four roles that change vanguard members could take. Governments would have the best of both worlds: highly-performing organizations continually being renewed by their third spaces.

DIGITAL HEDGEHOGS AND DIGITAL FOXES: AUTOMATION IN THE FEDERAL GOVERNMENT (2018)

In the latest update to the **President's Management Agenda**[ix], the Trump Administration is aggressively moving forward with its plans for automating federal government work. The Trump Administration estimates that five percent of federal jobs can be automated while 45 percent of the federal work activities could be automated across government. The goals of the President's Management Agenda are to "improve performance management, retrain workers, redeploy human capital, and simplify the hiring process."

One area in which federal government agencies are actively investigating automation is through *robotic process automation* (RPA). "Robotic process automation (RPA) is the application of technology that allows employees in a company to configure computer software or a "robot" to capture and interpret existing applications for processing a transaction, manipulating data, triggering responses and communicating with other digital systems."[x] The General Services Administration has identified 41 possible RPA candidates and is actively considering eight candidates for pilots ("What Federal Job Automation Looks Like" from the September 18, 2018 issue of *Federal Computing Week*).

If you are a professor who wants to introduce your students to RPA or a student who wants to teach themselves about RPA, you can download free RPA software to experiment with from **WorkFusion**. The software requires no knowledge of coding and provides plenty of tutorials. Public administration students can learn the power of RPA. Students can also realize the limits of automation.

Artificial Unintelligence

Meredith Broussard details the limits of artificial intelligence in *Artificial Unintelligence: How Computers Misunderstand the World*. One particularly compelling example of Broussard's book is a tutorial from the online data science site, Kaggle. Kaggle hosts data science contests from various organizations in which data scientists (amateur and professional) compete to create the best algorithms for cash prizes. To help prepare data scientists for the competitions, participants can download practice data sets to sharpen their data analytics skills.

One practice data set is the passenger list from the *Titanic*. The goal is to predict which passengers survived and which passengers died in the sinking of the *Titanic* using characteristics such as gender, type of ticket, and age. Broussard explains how to set up artificial intelligence routines to train an algorithm to determine who survived.

SPOILER ALERT – the characteristic that best predicts survivorship is the type of ticket. First class passengers have a better chance of survival versus passengers in steerage.

As Broussard points out, the prediction model built from the tutorial does a respectable job of predicting who survived. However, the model is not generalizable to determine who would survive in other ship sinking events because of the unique circumstances of the *Titanic*. Exceptional elements such as too few lifeboats, how one first officer misinterpreted the captain's orders on how to abandon ship, and other details not captured by the data. What is created is a model that is "overfitted" – an algorithm only suited for a particular data set. These artificial intelligence programs are "digital hedgehogs."

Why Experts Fail: Hedgehogs versus Foxes

In 1984, Dr. Philip Tetlock was appointed to the National Research Council of the National Academy of Sciences. He was part of a group devoted to discovering how to help the world avoid nuclear war. As he listened to experts on all sides of the political spectrum, Dr. Tetlock wondered how effective experts are in predicting the future. Over 27,450 predictions were collected from 284 experts as Dr. Tetlock tracked how well the experts predicted the future. The experts were no more effective at predicting events than random guessing.

Upon closer examination of the data, Dr. Tetlock found that a few experts did an excellent job in predicting future events. These experts were comfortable with complexity and uncertainty while constantly self-correcting their thinking and questioning their assumptions. Dr. Tetlock called these experts "foxes" from the ancient Greek poet's, Archilochus, poem. "The fox knows many things," the warrior-poet Archilochus wrote, "but the hedgehog knows one big thing" (Gardner, Daniel. *Future Babble* (p. 27)).

The experts who did the worse were the "hedgehogs." These experts are not comfortable with complexity and uncertainty. The hedgehogs attempt to create a core theoretical framework which the expert uses to reduce the amount of evidence to a few pieces of data. As Dr. Tetlock found, the political beliefs, level of education, and access to information made no difference in the accuracy of predictions. It was whether the expert's thinking style was a fox or hedgehog.

The Augmented Federal Workforce

In the quest to automate federal government work, remember the limits of artificial intelligence. When automating government processes, officials should consider how to utilize artificial intelligence best to augment human decision making. Automation can enhance decision making but should not replace humans in the decision process. That is because, at this stage of artificial intelligence technology, we can create useful digital hedgehogs – specialized algorithms effective at making good decisions in clearly defined environments. Artificial intelligence technology has yet to produce a digital hedgehog that can understand the nuances and complexities of dealing with citizens.

REINVENTING "REINVENTING GOVERNMENT" FOR THE DIGITAL TWIN AGE OF PUBLIC ADMINISTRATION (2018)

I started my government career as a paralegal in the Kentucky Natural Resources and Environmental Protection Cabinet on September 2, 1991. Thanks to an influential professor in college, I had become immersed in better management authors such as Peter Drucker and Tom Peters. During the spring and summer of 1991, I worked the third shift at a local convenience store while waiting to become hired in the Kentucky state government. It was during these many hours I would read the latest works on improving organizational management.

In 1992, David Osborne and Ted Gaebler published *Reinventing Government: How the Entrepreneurial Spirit is Transforming the Public Sector.* Having enjoyed Mr. Osborne's earlier book profiling innovative state governments (*Laboratories of Democracy,* 1988), I eagerly consumed *Reinventing Government* and tried to apply its lessons to my work at the Cabinet. A junior government paralegal talking about performance measures in a law office was strange but, I created some effective processes and methods using the newly acquired desktop PCs linked on a local area network.

Fast forward to six years later, and I was working on several National Performance Review projects as a Presidential Management Fellow at the General Services Administration. These were exciting times in government, and I was proud to be part of the performance revolution. However, as John Buntin in a recent article in *Governing* magazine asks, what happened to reinventing government in the last twenty-five years?[xi]

Mixed Results

Mr. Buntin's article is a good summary of the reinventing government efforts in the federal, state, and local governments. He recounts the successes and failures of the many reinvention projects to draw two important conclusions. The first conclusion is that even if a reinventing government project succeeds, it is hard to sustain.

The second conclusion is that many reinventing government projects were initiated by the executive branches and rarely considered the legislative branches' role in maintaining the project. As executive leadership and legislatures changed, the reinventing government projects lost their champions and critical people to maintain the projects.

However, Mr. Buntin's most important finding was how the emphasis on increasing performance results backfired on reinventing government. Rather than giving government managers the courage to be experimental and take risks, managers treated the new performance metrics as another compliance exercise. As Beth Blauer, head of the Maryland StateStat system, explains in the article, the focusing on the budget "automatically chilled innovative thinking." Agencies became "defensive" and concentrated on "justifying past performance" rather than "solving hard problems."

Going Lean

The performance management director for the Washington state government, Wendy Korthuis-Smith, argues for the bottom-up approach to performance management rather than the top-down reinventing government approach. Under the new framework, "Results Washington," five goal councils comprise 12 to 15 state agency directors. "The councils meet monthly to review data, discuss strategies, and collaborate on solutions," as recounted in Mr. Buntin's article. The Results Washington is an example of the lean approach in which the agencies partner with customers to help build and test solutions to meet the performance management challenges. Many other governments are experimenting with lean and design thinking to improve their performance management abilities and to deliver government services better.

The Resurgence of Reinventing Government?

Is it possible that reinventing government was too early? When I started my government career in 1991, we still had a typing pool of secretaries that would use the early word-processing software to turn our dictation cassettes into legal documents. In my work at the General Services Administration, I conducted one of the first surveys of how state and local governments were using the newly-commercialized World-Wide-Web to interact with their citizens. Collecting the information for feedback to help measure performance was admittedly more difficult back in the early 90s.

However, in the last twenty-five years, the ability to track performance data has become more effective and available. Often, frighteningly too effective and accessible. We are now entering an age where cognitive automation, artificial intelligence, and the Internet of Things can help us build "digital twins" of government agencies. Bernard Marr of *Forbes* magazine **defines a digital twin** as "a virtual model of a process, product or service. This pairing of the virtual and physical worlds allows analysis of data and monitoring of systems to head off problems before they even occur, prevent downtime, develop new opportunities and even plan for the future by using simulations."

Could using a lean and design thinking approach coupled with digital twin technologies, help governments reinvent themselves in a meaningful and sustainable way throughout changes in government leadership while responding to citizen's needs? It may be time to rethink how we reinvent government in this century.

BILL BRANTLEY

Transforming the Government Workforce

THE KEY TO GOVERNMENT EMPLOYEE ENGAGEMENT? LEARNING AND DEVELOPMENT (2015)

According to the latest Federal Employee Viewpoint Survey (EVS) results, Federal government employee morale is at its lowest point since the survey was initiated in 2003. "The government-wide employee engagement score is 57 out of 100, compared with the private sector's score of 72 out of 100," notes the *Washington Post* in the December 9, 2014 story, *"Federal workers' morale is at lowest point in years."* In every measure of workplace satisfaction, Federal employees ranked lower than their private sector counterparts. The one exception: Federal workers are more likely to enjoy their jobs.

Given the low morale and low engagement, it is odd that Federal workers state they enjoy their jobs. Ninety-six percent of employees will put in extra effort to accomplish their work according to the 2014 EVS. The 96% are willing to put in extra effort despite a majority that does not believe that they are paid fairly and that they receive sufficient recognition for their work. There is an intrinsic motivator behind why Federal workers enjoy their jobs. Understanding and enhancing this intrinsic motivator may have a positive spillover effect on the other aspects of employee engagement.

Learning and Development is the Key Intrinsic Motivator to Engagement

John Wiley and Sons, a book publishing company since 1807, improved employee engagement by 90% by creating a program to develop employee skills. Ty Hall explains in his February 12, 2015 blog posting, *"Increase Employee Engagement by Developing Employee Skills".*[xii]

Improving employee skills is an essential part of increasing employee engagement. If an employee's desire to advance in their career is not met, they will look for employment elsewhere. But when a focus is put on developing employee skills, the organization develops and grows.

Learning and Development in the Federal Government are Trending Downward

To test my assertion that learning and development are the intrinsic motivators for why Federal workers like their jobs, I examined the questions on the EVS that correspond to the employee's personal development and learning. For example, Question One: "I am given a real opportunity to improve my skills in my organization" that measures the employee's perception that opportunities for skill improvement exist in their workplace. The complete list of EVS questions I examined is 1, 2, 3, 8, 11, 18, 26, 27, and 68. Every question showed a downward trend from 2011 to 2014 (except for two questions that trended downward and then stayed flat from 2013 to 2014). Therefore, my assertion that learning and development are why Federal employees enjoyed their job is not because of the learning and development opportunities.

This cursory examination of learning and development EVS scores does point to another factor for the low morale and low engagement among Federal workers. How much of a factor depends on further analysis but given the Wiley case mentioned above and research from the Association for Talent Development (formerly the American Society for Training and Development) I argue that it is a significant factor - if not the most significant factor.

Attracting Millennials (and All Other Generations) Through Increased Learning and Development

In her 2006 book, *Retiring the Generation Gap: How Employees Young and Old Can Find Common Ground*, Jennifer Deal studied the generations from the Silent Generation (1925 to 1945) to the Late Xers (1977 to 1986). She found that all the generations had ten attitudes in common including "everyone wants to learn more than just about anything else" and "Almost everyone wants a coach." The Millennials were not included in this research, but it is safe to argue that they also would agree with a desire for development. "Millennial employees love training and development — and it's one of the top things they seek from their employers," writes Millennial Workplace Expert, Lindsey Pollack, in her January 30, 2015 blog posting, "How Training and Development Opportunities Boost Millennials' Employee Satisfaction."[xiii]

Why the Federal Government Needs to Focus on Learning and Development to Increase Employee Engagement

Senior Federal leaders are tasked with improving employee morale and engagement in the Federal workforce. Based on the arguments given above, increasing opportunities for learning and development would:

- Appeal to all the generations in the new multi-generational Federal workplace.

- Would significantly increase morale and engagement.

- Improve customer service due to better-trained and better-motivated employees.

- Improve government organizations.

- Robust learning and development programs would also help make the Federal government the employer of choice as students learn about the opportunities for personal growth and development in government service.

ONE POSSIBLE FUTURE FOR GOVERNMENT HUMAN RESOURCES MANAGEMENT (2015)

Nowadays, when I introduce myself at conferences and presentations, I claim to be an "accidental HR person." Like many other people who became "accidental project managers" or "accidental trainers," I stumbled into human resources (HR) because of my recent employment with the U.S. Office of Personnel Management. I was initially hired because of my IT development skills and my project management certification. As I continued to work in HR, I became intrigued by HR topics such as training and talent management. I am especially fascinated by how much HR has changed from purely transactional processes to becoming a vital strategic partner in organizations.

Bersin's People Management

One of my favorite thinkers in HR is Josh Bersin, who writes about the future of HR. Although his writings concern the evolution of HR in the private sector, many of his concepts apply just as well to the public sector. Recently, Bersin has been writing about the replacement of talent management by "people management."

He argues that the traditional talent management model of "hire to retire" does not reflect the new realities of work. Instead of hiring people that will stay with an organization and climb the corporate ladder to increasing responsibilities, many workers today act like professional athletes.

That is; workers stay with an organization if their work is satisfying and aligns with the worker's interests and development. Under the people management model, organizations need to focus on creating an engaging culture through good leadership that empowers workers.

Talent Imperatives for 2015

Bersin outlines nine imperatives for talent management.[xiv] The imperatives range from "improving management and leadership" to "delivering and managing [the] employment brand." Even though these imperatives were derived from studying private sector companies, the imperatives could easily apply to government agencies. Especially the imperatives that deal with increasing engagement improving the speed and quality of hire; accelerating time to competency/capability; and assessing and improving [the organization's] culture. I can see these imperatives reflected in the Federal Employment Viewpoint Survey (FEVS) results.

For example, according to the 2014 FEVS results, perceptions of senior leadership is at a five-year low. The low perception may have, at least in part, compelled President Obama to create the "People and Culture" part of the President's Management Agenda. The three sub-goals of "People and Culture' are:

(1) helping agencies create a culture of excellence and engagement that enables the highest possible performance from employees;

(2) assisting agencies in building a strong, world-class Federal management team, beginning with the Senior Executive Service (SES); and

(3) helping agencies to draw from all segments of society to ensure that they hire the best talent.

The sub-goals reflect most of Bersin's talent imperatives; especially with improving leadership, innovating hiring practices, and increasing engagement among the Federal workforce. I could easily see the sub-goals growing to encompass all nine of Bersin's talent imperatives. *(In the interests of full disclosure, I worked with a team on the engagement portion of the "People and Culture" and also contributed toward the "GovConnect" project.)*

The Simply Irresistible Agency*

[*Bersin uses "The Simple Irresistible Organization" which is a registered trademark.]

To support the new people management model, Bersin has created an organizational model that best attracts the new workers: the Simply Irresistible Organization®. The Simply Irresistible Organization® model comprises five major themes: meaningful work; hands-on management; positive work environment; growth opportunities; and trust in leadership. Under each theme are supporting tools and methods to build a high-engagement and high-worker-empowerment organization. According to Bersin, many modern successful companies such as Google and Apple already practice the five major themes.

These same five major themes can also help to create simply irresistible government agencies. According to the FEVS, many government workers agree that their work is meaningful, and that drives their engagement. Also, many government employees give high scores to their immediate supervisors; thus, two of the five themes are already in place. What remains is to improve the work environments of agencies while increasing growth opportunities and trust in senior leadership. The People and Culture sub-goals seem to be in the right direction to building simply irresistible federal agencies.

The Future of Government People Management

As the title suggests, this is just one possible future for government HR management. I am not advocating that governments merely adopt all Bersin's work because the public sector has constraints and advantages not found in the private sector. However, the talent imperatives of improving leadership, innovating hiring practices, and increasing engagement toward creating simply irresistible government workplaces is where government HR management should be heading. Workplace realities have changed, and governments also need to change their approaches to managing their people.

TIME FOR A COMMUNITY OF PRACTICE ON GOVERNMENT PROGRAM AND PROJECT MANAGEMENT? (2016)

In September, the U.S. House of Representatives passed a bill to improve the Federal government's management of programs and projects. The U.S. Senate is expected to approve the House bill soon, and President Obama has expressed his eagerness to sign the final bill into law. The Program Management Improvement and Accountability Act of 2015 (PMIAA) will revolutionize how the Federal government plans and executes program and project management in four ways:

1. Establishing a formal job series for Federal program managers.

2. Creating a government-wide program management policy.

3. Designating a senior executive in each Federal agency who will oversee that agency's program management policy and strategy.

4. Instituting an interagency council on program management.

What led to one of the few bipartisan-supported policies in this Congressional session? Some point to the recent failure of Healthcare.Gov while others argue that the 25-year history of the General Accountability Office's High-Risk List consistently points to the need for better program management. Per a report by the National Academy of Public Administration (NAPA), an annual one percent increase in program efficiency will save nearly a trillion dollars in the next ten years. [xv]

The Current State of Federal Project and Program Management

The Project Management Institute (PMI) sponsored the NAPA report to persuade the Federal government to improve project management and program management. As PMI explains, programs comprise many related projects. Improve the management of projects and program management will also improve. The NAPA report found five issues with Federal government project management and program management.

First, there are no holistic laws and policies for program management. Laws and policies were passed to handle specific program management problems without an overall framework. Second, program management is not perceived as "essential to government performance, success, and results" (quoting the NAPA report). Third, agency management is not aware of their roles and responsibilities about the proper administration of programs and projects. Fourth, the training and development of program managers and project managers are inconsistent and inadequate. Fifth, and finally, there is no professional community of Federal government project managers and program managers. A professional community can help Federal project and program managers to mentor each other and advocate for professional development initiatives.

An Opportunity for the Public Administration Education Community

For the last three years, I have been a moderator for the Federal government sessions at the University of Maryland's Center for Project Management Excellence's Project Management Symposium. I have recruited presenters and have managed an all-day track devoted to issues in Federal government project management. We have had a range of presentations from traditional project management techniques for government facilities to cutting-edge agile project management methods used by the U.S. Digital Service and the Presidential Innovation Fellows. There are pockets of innovative and effective project management offices doing some great work in delivering government services and improving agency processes.

Each year, the participants remark how they wish they knew about the other projects and the work that other agencies are doing. Most participants are members of PMI and network through that organization but, sometimes feel lost in the sheer size of PMI and the project management community. Also, the project management and program management environment in government has enough differences that some private sector practices do not apply.

For example, many government projects and programs suffer from inconsistent budgeting. The annual budgeting cycle limits the ability to forecast and plan programs that are multiyear in focus and execution. With the environment of continuing resolutions on the Federal government level, program managers and project managers are forced to keep the programs and projects in maintenance mode. Maintaining current projects and programs prevents using state-of-art program and project management methods such as agile project management. Thus, government program and project managers are eager to learn about the newest ways but need methods that can work in the unique environment of public administration.

Many public administration education schools teach program management and project management. However, in my observation, some schools do not incorporate lessons on the latest techniques and management methods such as human-centered design, lean startup, and agile project management. Public administration schools are in a unique position to study the effectiveness of modern management methods in improving government program and project management. Another great resource that public administration schools have is their research. However, that research needs to be translated into actionable suggestions for government practitioners.

G-PPMI: Government Program/Project Management Institute

Maybe this is the time for the academic community and the practitioner community to come together in a new organization. A community of practice that connects the government program and project managers to share best practices and lesson learned. This community of practice will also serve as a way for public administration academics to find rich areas for future research projects while making their current research accessible to practitioners. There is a need as evidenced by the NAPA report and, once the PMIAA is enacted, there will be an interagency council on program management. Perfect time for the government community to raise their voices.

BRINGING PUBLIC ADMINISTRATION PRACTITIONERS AND ACADEMICS TOGETHER THROUGH PROJECT BASED RESEARCH (2016)

On August 31, 2016, *Governing* posted an article by Dr. Philip Joyce in which he argued that academia is failing government:[xvi]

The academic disciplines of public administration and public policy developed because of a need for problem-focused, interdisciplinary fields whose raison d'etre was the development and dissemination of knowledge that could improve both government and society. If we genuinely want our research to matter, we as academics must embrace measures focused on actual policy and practical management concerns rather than continuing to reward ourselves for talking to each other.

Dr. Joyce focused on how public administration scholars created research based on increasing the impact factor of their research as measured by how often their journal articles were cited by other scholars. The journal impact factor leads to scholars only talking to each other rather than being rewarded for developing solutions that practitioners can benefit. As Dr. Joyce points out, "[research] products that might result in a broader impact -- op-eds, blog posts, shorter pieces in trade publications, or testimony before state or local governing bodies -- not only do not count for tenure but are viewed as detracting from the real work: publishing for other academics."

Is the Business School Model Appropriate for Public Administration Schools?

In response to Dr. Joyce's article, Howard Risher argued that business schools would be a good model for public administration schools to disseminate research to practitioners.[xvii] According to Mr. Risher, "The private sector has the advantage that new companies with new organizational strategies are always emerging." The successful policies and practices are then "discussed at conferences and in articles." The business schools then research the newly successful strategies and practices to "[confirm] or [debunk] the value of [the] new ideas."

Risher supports his argument by discussing how the Office of Personnel Management has used "demo projects" to test new Federal human resources policies. A more recent example, not mentioned by Risher, is the use of lean startup principles to create the Consumer Financial Protection Board. Other Federal agencies, such as the Department of Justice and Health and Human Services, have used innovation labs to test and implement new policy innovations.

However, what is the ratio of successful business innovations to failed business innovations? What is the actual cost in failed business innovations? According to some statistics about business startups, only five percent of new businesses survive after five years. There are also numerous examples of business movements that looked successful at first but, ultimately failed. The reengineering movement of the early 1990s is a classic example. Innovating first and researching later seem too risky of a strategy for the public sector.

Is Project-Based Learning a Solution for Connecting Academics with Practitioners?

According to the Buck Institute for Education, a leading research institution in project-based learning, project-based learning is: "a teaching method in which students gain knowledge and skills by working for an extended period to investigate and respond to an authentic, engaging and complex question, problem, or challenge." The advantages of project-based learning for students is the sustained inquiry into a challenging problem which allows the student to create a public product demonstrating their knowledge while providing a useful, innovative contribution.

The benefit to academics is they will be introduced to a public administration challenge through the mentoring of their students. The academic can aid the practitioners by providing research that applies to the problem that is the focus of the project-based learning. Academics will then benefit by giving the study a real-world test and exploring new avenues for future research. Meanwhile, the practitioners benefit from having a new policy innovation or solution supported by rigorous analysis. All parties benefit from the dialogue surrounding the public administration students' project.

Project-Based Research

It is not always necessary to have a student project to bring academics and practitioners together in a mutually beneficial collaboration. There are plenty of opportunities in the current challenges facing local, state, and national governments.

For example, I mentioned in last month's column that Congress is ready to pass legislation to improve how the government manages programs and projects. President Obama will most likely sign the legislation into law so there will be plenty of opportunities for the academic and practitioner community to work together.

There is much valuable research on government project and program management that most practitioners are not aware of but, would appreciate. Academics have an excellent opportunity for their work to have a real impact factor on the public agencies they study.

A MISSED OPPORTUNITY? GOVERNMENT HUMAN CAPITAL UNDER THE TRUMP ADMINISTRATION (2017)

If President Trump's actions are any indication, the Federal government's workforce will face significant changes that may be detrimental to government workers. First, the hiring freeze is predicated on President Trump's belief that the government workforce has too many employees. There is some dispute over whether the Federal workforce is too large but, the freeze is only the first step.

Newt Gingrich, an informal advisor to President Trump, has advocated reforming the Federal workforce as the new administration's primary goal. Specifically, making it easier to fire Federal workers who do not cooperate with the new cabinet secretaries and their policies. Adding to this, the Congress has resurrected an old rule that allows Congress to reduce the salary of a specific government worker. These actions are the wrong way to make the Federal government more effective and efficient.

President Trump ran on the platform that, being a successful businessman, he can bring the best business thinking of running the government. If so, President Trump may want to consider some of the best business thinking on human capital trends. For the last several years, Bersin by Deloitte has published a study on global human capital trends. These are the best human capital practices that are used by many successful businesses. I have picked three from the 2016 report that is most applicable to the government.

Networks of Teams

The first trend is the move away from hierarchical structures to more fluid, team-based structures that can adapt and innovate rapidly. New team-based structures are necessary because of the fast-changing and complex environments that surround private sector organizations. Organizations are creating "networks of teams" which emphasize high empowerment, strong communication, and rapid information flow. Teams make their own decisions and set their own goals in pursuit of the organization's strategic goals. Pushing decision authority down to the team level allows the teams to "deliver results faster, engage people better, and stay closer to their mission (from the Deloitte report).

Arguably, governments face even more complex and fast-changing environments which require innovative and quick actions. Nurturing networks of teams within agencies can be an effective way to reform how agencies deliver on their missions. Building networks of teams is relatively easy to implement reform that can have significant payoffs.

Leaders at All Levels

The Federal government concentrates on leadership development with programs devoted to making better supervisors, mid-level managers, and Senior Executive Service leaders. However, there are only a few agencies that work on developing the leadership abilities of all the agency's workforce. The U.S. Patent and Trademark Office (USPTO) has an extensive leadership training program for the agency employees no matter what their job role is. The USPTO's comprehensive leadership training program reflects the private industry's human capital trend to increase leadership training as organizations switch to networks of teams. Private organizations have also invested heavily in succession planning which requires identifying and training potential leaders.

So, what leadership skills are organizations concentrating on? First, the ability to collaborate across organizational silos and between organizations. The second ability is to develop and implement innovative solutions while the third ability is becoming motivational team leaders. For Federal agencies, the traditional command-and-control leadership style is giving way to servant leadership as more emphasis is placed on increasing government employee engagement. As some agencies have found, fostering leadership development is an effective way of increasing employee engagement.

Employee-Lead Learning

Training and development are undergoing a fundamental change because of the Internet and the need for employees to keep acquiring new skills. Traditional training methods in which the organization's training department decided what employees needed to learn, created the training and delivered the programs at the convenience of the training department no longer works. Thanks to online training providers, online academic programs, and free tutorials on YouTube, employees can take any training when and where they want. As the Deloitte report observes, employees realize that continual learning is the key to moving up in his or her career and therefore are demanding more training from their organizations.

Leading organizations are turning their training departments into "learning experience architects" as trainers become curators who pull together existing training assets (both internal and external to the organization) into online personalized learning systems. Learners can then create individualized learning paths that comprise formal classroom learning, social learning interactions with peers, and self-paced online training. The training department provides a better learner experience for employees while helping the organization to achieve its strategic goals through increased employee development.

Seizing the Opportunity

Instead of focusing on the size of the Federal government, the Trump Administration should focus on the quality of service from the Federal government. Government agencies do an excellent job of delivering value and services to the American public. However, there is room for improvement. Not all successful business practices apply to government but, some methods can revitalize and reform government operations. People are the heart of organizational success and improving human capital processes improves the organization overall.

ESTABLISHING EFFECTIVE GOVERNMENT PROGRAM AND PROJECT MANAGEMENT OFFICES (2017)

As the Office of Management and Budget (OMB) works on implementing the Program Management Improvement and Accountability Act (PMIAA), Federal agencies are considering how to incorporate PMIAA into their agency programs and processes. Many agencies have pockets of program management excellence, but the real challenge is connecting the isolated pockets to improve program management of the Federal government overall.

I recently presented on government program and project management offices at the University of Maryland's 2017 Project Management Symposium. I am researching the current state of the Federal agencies' program and project management offices. My purpose is to determine the number and structure of the Federal program and project management offices. My research will establish a baseline to measure the impact of PMIAA. There is much research on the benefits of project management offices in the private sector but few empirical studies on government project management offices. Two studies provide insights into how to implement PMIAA.

What Makes a Project Management Office Successful?

Dai and Wells (2004) conducted a study to determine which of the project management office services correlated most highly with project performance. The researchers studied these project management services:

- Project support to offload administrative burdens such as reporting and software operations from project managers.

- Consulting and mentoring, whereby professional PM expertise such as proposal development and project planning is provided.

- Development and enforcement of standards and methods to leverage best practices and to ensure members of the organization are all "speaking the same PM language."

- Training to enhance individual skills and to encourage professional certification.

- Assisting in staffing projects with project managers.

- Playing a high-tech project support role by enabling virtual project offices across geographical and organizational distance.

Of all the services offered by the project management office, two services were found to highly correlate with project management success. The first is the establishment of project management standards and methods. Project management offices that create manage and maintain organization-wide standards, tools and practices have the most impact on the organization's project successes.

The second service is the knowledge management function. Project management organizations that keep and disseminate lessons learned also increases the organization's project successes. These two services are closely related as the lessons learned help refine the project management organization's set of standards and practices.

Can Private Sector Best Practices Be Successfully Transferred to Government Project Management Offices?

The previous study offers a path for creating a successful project management office in government. However, how well do private sector project management practices translate into the public sector? Shah, Khan, and Khalil (2011) studied that very question when they conducted a case study of Pakistan's Electronic Government Directorate. According to their research, ten significant differences specific to the government makes it difficult to transplant private sector best practices:

- Monopolistic in nature

- Lack of adequate and appropriate skills within the public sector

- Larger number of stakeholders, often with conflicting interests

- Elaborate bureaucratic processes of projects approval, funds release, reporting, and monitoring

- More significant, and more complex, projects

- Sometimes ambiguous goals, or goals not adequately linked with organizational (i.e., national development) goals

- Extensive external dependencies and influences, i.e., from politicians, citizens, external funding agencies, etc.

- Diluted personal responsibilities and accountability, sometimes drive by the attitude of 'passing the buck.'

- Shorter planning and financial horizons (or perspectives)

- Subject to laws, regulations, and oversight that exceed those of private organizations

Because of these differences, the researchers advise that government agencies pay close attention to training the agency workforce in program and project management, establishing organization-wide standards and practices, and investigating delays and problems. Then, when adopting a best practice, rethink how the best practice will operate in the government environment. The agency should carefully monitor the progress of the best practice and use a robust lessons-learned process to refine the best practice continually.

The Profound Potential Impact of PMIAA

PMIAA may have just as much impact (if not more) on the Federal government's ability to deliver services. Reforming government has been a consistent aim of many Presidential administrations with mixed results. Part of the problem with improving government is that attempting to transplant best practices without considering the unique environment of government reduces the usefulness of the best practices.

PMIAA is different because reforms are already established in the agencies' pockets of excellence. PMIAA's contribution is to help build program and project management capacity among the Federal workforce, create governmentwide standards, and establish a governmentwide council to spread best practices. As the research shows, these are the correct steps to creating high-performance program and project management offices.

THE IMPACT OF MILLENNIALS, GENERATION Z, AND GENERATION A ON THE FEDERAL WORKFORCE (2017)

In the last national election, the earliest born members of Generation Z voted for the first time. In 2019, the American workforce will see the influx of tens of millions of Gen Zers who, according to some researchers, will be a stark contrast to the Millennials that will make the most substantial part of the 2020 workforce. According to **one** researcher's study of Gen Z,[xviii] this generational group has seven distinguishing traits:

1. **Phigital** – To the Gen Zers, the physical and digital worlds have been merged. Ninety-one percent of Gen Zers want to work for technologically-sophisticated organizations.

2. **Hyper-Custom** – Gen Zers want to customize everything from the products they buy to the careers they work.

3. **Realistic** – The Great Recession of 2008 and 9/11 have taught Gen Z to not take their future for granted.

4. **Fear of Missing Out [FOMO]** – Social media has helped Gen Z to be on top of all trends. However, the acceleration of social media trends leaves Gen Z fearful of missing out on the latest news and events.

5. **Weconomists** – Gen Z has grown up with shared economy companies like Uber and Airbnb. Gen Z doesn't like silos.

6. **DIY** – Like Generation X, Generation Z has a strong independent streak.

7. **Driven** – This group is very competitive and may not so easily collaborate as Millennials do.

I approach generational studies with skepticism. However, I am intrigued by the early findings of this researcher. Other researchers also support the **pragmatic and ultra-competitiveness traits of Gen**

Z. Of all the research I have read, the research on the **digital habits of Gen Z is most intriguing.**[xix]

"Yes, this generation communicates almost entirely through screens and not always with actual words (GIFs, videos, and emoji also do the trick). Gen-Z'ers are less idealistic and more thrifty than millennials, having grown up in the twin shadows of the recession and student debt crisis. When it comes to privacy on social media sites such as Instagram, Snapchat, Tumblr or Twitter, the survey showed that teens are far less guarded than millennials and Gen X members. Members of Gen Z think that everyone should get a smartphone at age 13 and that it is acceptable to use it basically anywhere — at a family dinner, during a religious service, even at weddings (even their own weddings, the survey shows.)"

At the same time, Generation Z is entering the workforce; the workforce is undergoing a major transformation – artificially intelligent (AI) automation. We have seen the increasing use of chatbots and AI robots. There are predictions that AI automation will **take away jobs leading to massive unemployment** while there are other predictions that AI automation **will create new economic opportunities.** Some jobs will be lost by AI automation, but that may be for the better as it will free up humans to work in creative and more satisfying jobs. What appears to happen now is the rise of the augmented workforce. In 2017, **"41 percent of companies reported they have fully implemented or have made significant progress in adopting cognitive and AI technologies within their workforce while 34% more companies are beginning to adopt augmentation technologies."**[xx]

Imagine the intersection of Generation Z (which is the most digitally-ready generation in American history) with "Generation A" (A for augmented, artificial (intelligence), or automated). How will the new workplace AI technologies amplify the workforce tendencies of all the generations and especially Generation Z?

As a developer and deliverer of leadership development training in a federal agency, I am seeing a higher demand for more soft skills training among the younger employees. Younger federal employees are also demanding shorter training courses that are mobile-friendly and provide just-in-time skills training.

What does the merger of Generation Z with Generation A mean for federal agencies as 2020 rapidly approaches? How will current federal managers (Baby Boomers, Generation X, and Millennials) adapt to Generation Z behaviors and attitudes? How will federal agencies use augmentation technologies and AI-driven automation in delivering government services?

We are only a few short years from 2020 which promises profound changes in the U.S. federal government and for the American public.

THREE SKILLS TO HELP YOU KEEP YOUR GOVERNMENT CAREER IN THE AGE OF AUTOMATION (2017)

According to a recent United Kingdom government report, "[a]utomation could replace 250,000 jobs in government over the next 10 to 15 years — with potentially one million more under threat."[xxi] There is no comparable US federal government study but, most federal, state and local government jobs are also at risk of being automated. If your government job is routine, follows a well-defined process, and rarely changes, an artificial intelligence (AI) agent could easily replace you.

 So, how do you as a government worker, remain irreplaceable? One way is to master these three skills. It will be some time before AI agents can learn these skills sufficiently to replace humans.

Strategic Thinking – One advantage that humans have over AI agents is the ability to find solutions to novel situations. The human advantage for novel solutions is because of how AI agents are created. AI agents use deep learning to think through situations. Deep learning uses massive sets of data from past events to help AI agents to create problem-solving models. Therefore, AI agents are often better at making medical diagnoses and handling insurance claims. As long as there are plenty of data to draw upon, AI agents will excel at learning from experience.

However, in situations with little information to go on or the data is conflicted, AI agents cannot create useful problem-solving models. The inability to useful problem-solving models is especially true when dealing with volatile, uncertainty, complexity, and ambiguity (VUAC) situations. Humans have an innate ability to combine concepts from disparate fields to create novel solutions. A classic example is how Philo Farnsworth created the idea of television by reimagining how he plowed a field to the way a cathode ray tube uses scan lines to paint a picture on a screen.

Communication – Chatbots are the newest innovation with Google's Siri and Amazon's Alexa. The chatbots are becoming better at interpreting questions and creating answers. However, chatbots still cannot fully interact with humans who pepper their language with humor and hidden meanings. Put a chatbot into a situation where a behavioral script follows and chatbots excel. Think of how you behave in a restaurant.

There is an understood script we all follow such as placing an order, interacting with the server, and paying the bill at the end. Intentions are clear, and interactions follow a typical pattern.

Compare the scripted communications to situations where the situation is new, and the script is written as the participants interact. Much of human combines verbal and nonverbal communication. What may seem like a straightforward verbal interaction can be altered by the nonverbal signals surrounding the verbal statements.

Improving your skills in oral communication, written communication, and emotional intelligence will give you the edge over AI chatbots.

Teambuilding – One skill not automated is teambuilding. Teams are also a new way to build high-performing organizations. Again, the rise of the VUAC world has compelled the need for organizational agility and quick action. Per General McChrystal, teams and teams of teams are the best way to handle the demands of the VUAC world. A good skill to acquire and refine is the ability to build and lead teams; even teams of humans and AI agents.

If your government job is routine and dull, it may be a blessing it becomes automated. However, this doesn't mean you need to lose your job. Automating your job can be the signal you need to upgrade yourself and your skills to find more satisfying work. Use these three skills to propel your government career forward into a better future.

(Originally appeared in *GovLoop*)

THE SIMPLY IRRESISTIBLE
MULTIGENERATIONAL GOVERNMENT AGENCY
(2017)

I first heard about the generational profiles in an undergraduate communication course on persuasion. It was 1988, and our professor played a training video he had borrowed from a Fortune 500 company. He never told us about the company.

The video featured a single presenter in front of whiteboard with these generations on a timeline: Silent Generation (1920s to 1945); Early Baby Boomers (1946 to 1954); Late Baby Boomers (1955 to 1963); Early Xers (1964 to 1976); and Late Xers (1977 to 1986). Everyone in my class came from the Early Xers. The presenter described the significant events that shaped the values and attitudes of each generation. It was compelling although, I was dubious as to how the presenter generalized the generations.

Since then, I've been to several presentations on the generations, and I still carry the same skepticism. When I was a PMF, I attended training at the General Services Administration that talked about how to manage Generation X.

Recently, I read an article on how to manage Millennials, and it sounded just like the Generation X presentation. Of all the research I have read on the generations, I am most influenced by Dr. Jennifer Deal's book. In *Retiring the Generation Gap: How Employees Young and Old Can Find Common Ground*, Dr. Deal surveyed over 5,800 people to determine their generational attitudes. From this research, she derived ten principles:

1. "All generations have similar values; they just express them differently. The number one consistent value is family with love, integrity, and spirituality in the top four."

2. "Everyone wants respect; they just don't define it the same way."

3. "Trust matters."

4.   "People want leaders who are credible and trustworthy."

5.   "Organizational politics is a problem – no matter how old (or young) you are."

6.   "No one really likes change."

7.   "Loyalty depends on the context, not on the generation."

8.   "It's as easy to retain a young person as an older one – if you do the right things."

9.   "Everyone wants to learn – more than just about anything else."

10.   "Almost everyone wants a coach."

What is especially interesting about these principles is how they reinforce recent research in employee engagement. Josh Bersin (from Bersin by Deloitte) has been researching the drivers of employee engagement. After a two-year, worldwide research project, Bersin developed the model for the Simply Irresistible Organization in which he describes the five elements that drive engagement. These elements are each supported by four factors:

Meaningful Work - Autonomy; Selection to Fit; Small Teams; and Time for Slack

Supportive Management - Clear Goal Setting; Coaching and Feedback; Leadership Development; and Modern Performance Management

Fantastic Environment - Flexible and Humane Work Environment; Recognition Rich Culture; Open and Flexible Work Spaces; Inclusive and Diverse Culture

Growth Opportunity - Facilitated Talent Mobility; Career Growth in Many Paths; Self and Formal Development; and High Impact Learning Culture

Trust in Leadership - Mission and Purpose; Investment in People and Trust; Tranparency and Communication; and Inspiration

Notice how the intergenerational principles are interwoven into the Simply Irresistible Organization (SIO) framework. Thus, government organizations that adopt the SIO framework will also create an attractive multigenerational workplace. This assertion makes sense as the problem with employee engagement cuts across the generations and many organizations.

Per a recent national poll,[xxii] the private sector and local government have the highest employee engagement numbers with 44% of employees reporting they are engaged at work. For the federal government, only 34% of employees are engaged, while only 29% of state government employees feel engaged. Things in government need to change. Reinventing government agencies with the SIO framework is an excellent direction to go.

So, what about the Millennials? Why haven't I talked about the Millennials and their workplace needs? In the next chapter, I will discuss Dr. Deal's recent book: *What Millennials Want from Work: How to Maximize Engagement in Today's Workforce.* How do Millennials feel about the five elements of the SIO framework?

(Originally appeared in *GovLoop*)

BEING SIMPLY IRRESISTIBLE TO MILLENNIALS: SOME THOUGHTS FOR FEDERAL AGENCIES (2017)

In my last chapter, I wrote about the simply irresistible multigenerational government agency. Starting with Dr. Jennifer Deal's research into the silent generation, baby boomers, and generation X, I listed the ten principles she discovered in her study. Essentially:

1.   All generations have similar values, and all generations want respect.

2.   Trust matters.

3.   Loyalty is contextual and not generational.

4.   Everyone wants to learn and be coached.

I then compared these findings to Josh Bersin's Simply Irresistible Organization (SIO). The five elements of the SIO (meaningful work, great management, fantastic environment, growth opportunities, and trust in leadership) fulfill the ten principles of the silent generation, baby boomers, and generation X.

What about millennials?

In 2016, Dr. Deal and Alec Levenson released *What Millennials Want From Work: How To Maximize Engagement in Today's Workforce*. The authors collected 25,000 survey responses from millennials and 29,000 survey responses from older workers in 22 countries between 2008 and 2015. I especially found the reactions from the older generations to be helpful as it placed the millennial answers into context. The authors then use the research to address five points about millennials.

Point One – Millennials are both entitled and hardworking

Millennials are often accused of demanding perks and privileges at work, are sloppy in their communications, and don't want to do the necessary but routine work. Millennials will put in the long hours, do the required work, and understand hard work is essential to moving up. They are similar to the other generations in this way. What may be the issue is that millennials will speak their mind and love to find ways to "hack work."

Point Two – Millennials strongly want learning and development opportunities

Millennials are, on the average, the unhappiest of the generations. Millennials face higher student loan debt and an uncertain job market. Millennials realize that they are disposable to their organizations and the best way to keep working is continual reskilling. Therefore, millennials want to work in organizations where they can keep learning and are encouraged to develop. The other generations also want to learn and improve continually. However, millennials seem less trusting of their organizations than the other generations.

Point Three – Millennials want to do good and well

When I started a full-time job after leaving college, I immediately signed up for a retirement account. Retirement planning so early in my career was considered unusual among my Generation X peers but, I would have been right at home with the Millennials. Millennials want to work in jobs that have meaning and a positive impact on the world. Millennials also want to make enough to escape the burden of debt most have and to have a comfortable retirement. Compensation and retirement planning is a shared concern among the generations but seems more intense with millennials.

Point Four – Millennials are high-tech and high-touch

All the generations want friends at work and a sense of community. Probably the second most consistent reason that people leave a job is that he or she felt "alone." This reason is close to the top reason people leave a job – because of their relationship with their boss. Millennials, on average, use social media more than the other generations. There is not that much difference between social media usage by generations. Millennials are quicker to experiment with new technologies which can be both beneficial to the organization and dangerous. Useful because this helps the organization stay innovative; dangerous in that new technologies can expose organizations to new security risks.

Point Five – Millennials are committed until they are not

Like the other generations, millennials are committed to their work teams and will contribute their fullest. However, millennials are also more likely to be convinced that better opportunities are out there and thus, more easily lured away by recruiters.

Remember, this is the generation most concerned about their financial future and ability to compete in the workplace. Many millennials have yet to learn the hard way that a new opportunity is not always better. Every generation before the millennials learned that lesson the hard way. Personally, it took two hard lessons for me to stop jumping on new opportunities rather than try to improve my existing job.

Given these five points, the Simply Irresistible Organization is a perfect match for millennials. The SIO builds community through the small work teams and provides a good work-life balance through slack time. There is continual trust building between management and the employees which speak to the millennials' need for security.

Finally, the high-impact learning culture will meet the millennials' needs for continual reskilling, mentoring, and coaching. Thus, if government agencies want to attract millennials, the agencies should adopt the SIO model. SIO is good for millennials and also will benefit the other generations.

(Originally appeared in *GovLoop*)

HOW ORGANIZATIONAL DRAG IS WASTING THE TIME, TALENT, AND ENERGY OF YOUR AGENCY'S WORKFORCE (2017)

People are the most valuable strategic assets in any organization. As Homer Simpson might say, "well, duh!" However, many senior organizational leaders are realizing that the time, talent, and energy of their workforce makes the organization successful.

As Michael Mankins and Eric Garton explain in *Time, Talent, and Energy: Overcome Organizational Drag and Unleash Your Team's Productive Power*, executives used to concentrate on financial decisions. Finance was important because financial capital was a scarce resource in the industrial age companies. It took much money to build a railroad, a factory, or a laboratory. However, capital is abundant in today's knowledge age.

Not so abundant in the knowledge age are the innovative ideas that help organizations succeed. The innovative ideas are, as Mankins and Garton write, "the product of individuals and teams who have the time to work productively, who have the skills they need to make a difference, and who bring creativity and enthusiasm to their jobs." The best way to help the individuals and teams produce innovative ideas is to manage their time, talent, and energy better. Thus, senior leadership needs to focus on better managing human capital by reducing organizational drag.

Organizational drag is familiar to anyone who has worked in organizations. Essentially, organizational drag is the cumulative effect of "needless internal interactions, unproductive or inconsequential meetings, and unnecessary e-communications." Organizational drag wastes time and saps the energy of the workforce. It is not the fault of the employees they are not productive. Instead, senior leaders need to remove these common organizational barriers to the employees' time, talents, and energy.

Time

In the 1970s, an executive received up to 5,000 communications per year. In the 2010s, executives can expect to receive 50,000 communications per year. Meeting time has also grown to where 15% of the workforce's time is spent in meetings.

Ironically, all of these meetings and communications has increased the number of organizational silos because most interactions are informational and take place within departments rather than collaborative and across organizational units. "If all the e-communications and meetings were bunched up at the beginning of the week, [the employee] wouldn't be able to start other work until late Thursday afternoon."

Talent

I didn't entirely agree with Mankins and Garton on dividing up the workforce into the "difference makers" and the rest of the workforce. I believe with the proper coaching and development; all employees can be difference makers.

However, I do agree that organizations do not think strategically about how they build work teams that take the best advantage of the skills of the employees. Team building is still a lost art for many organizations.

Energy

Mankins and Garton suggest a pyramid of employee needs to help increase employee engagement in organizations. Like Maslow's hierarchy of needs, there are basic things that companies can do to make employees feel satisfied with their jobs. Once employees are satisfied, organizations can then help employees feel engaged. Once employees are engaged, organizations can then strive to help employees feel inspired. It will take much work to help bring employees from satisfied to inspired so, what is the payoff?

A satisfied employee is 40% more productive than an unsatisfied employee. An engaged employee is 44% is more productive than a satisfied employee. However, an inspired employee is 125% is more productive than a satisfied employee! Imagine, if you have a team of ten satisfied employees. If you could turn each of the team members into inspired employees, you would have the productivity of a team of 25 employees without additional salary costs.

Increasing Organizational Thrust and Reducing Organizational Drag

Mankins and Garton do not use the term "organizational thrust;" I coined it from the aeronautical concepts of drag and thrust. If organizations can better manage the time and talent of their workforce, then organizations will increase the energy of their workforce.

A workforce of merely satisfied employees who become a workforce of 100% inspired employees will produce tremendous organizational thrust. The organizational thrust increases the number of innovative ideas and the difference makers to implement those ideas.

To measure the organizational drag in your organization, take the diagnostic at www.timetalentenergy.com. What are ideas that you have in reducing organizational drag and increasing organizational thrust in your agency?

(Originally appeared in *GovLoop*)

DEVELOPING NEW LEADERS FOR HEALTHY AND AGILE PUBLIC AGENCIES (2018)

In my work at the U.S. Patent and Trademark Office's Enterprise Training Division, I have led the Aspiring Leader and Individual Leader program and lead the Supervisor Certification Program. I work with leadership theory and leadership development theory daily.

I have been involved with leadership theory and practice since I was a teenager in the Boy Scouts. I have held leadership roles in government agencies, nonprofits, and in dot-com startups. I have been exposed to much leadership theory while pursuing a master's in political management, an MBA in project management, and a Ph.D. in public policy and management.

I have watched organizations dramatically change with the impact of the Internet and digital transformation. These experiences are why I studied how leadership and leadership development have changed in the age of digital organizations.

Leadership and Its Importance in Organizational Health, Organizational Agility, and Employee Engagement.

Between 2013 and 2015, I worked as an analyst for the U.S. Office of Personnel Management's (OPM) Strategic Workforce Planning Group. I was tasked with determining how to measure the organizational health of a government agency. This assignment led to an extensive study of the organizational health concept which then branched out into the organizational agility concept. I was working on employee engagement research.

 During my OPM work, I saw connections between organizational health, organizational agility, and employee engagement. A common factor in all three areas is the central importance of leadership. I asked what type of leadership is needed to create and lead a healthy and agile organization with high employee engagement while successfully delivering on its mission. This question has led to an intensive five-year study of leadership development.

The HASIO Organizational Model

I used three models to define organizational health, organizational agility, and employee engagement. For organizational health, I used McKinsey's Organizational Health Index (*Beyond performance: How great organizations build an ultimate competitive advantage,* 2011). Organizational agility comes from Worley, Williams, and Lawler's work (*The agility factor: Building adaptable organizations for superior performance,* 2014). The employee engagement model comes the research of Josh Bersin who terms his model the **"Simply Irresistible Organization."** The models complement each other well, and I have combined the models into the "Healthy, Agile, Simply Irresistible Organization" (HASIO). At the heart of the HASIO model and interwoven through the model are various leadership characteristics.

The HASIO Leadership Model

Thirteen characteristics in the HASIO Leadership Model are organized around three primary organizational health functions. The first organizational health function, "internal alignment to the organization's mission and vision," has five leadership characteristics:

- Goal Setting and Vision

- Communication

- Inspiration

- Transparency

- Trust-Building

The second organizational health function is the "quality of execution of the organization's business processes." The four leadership characteristics that enable a high quality of execution are:

- Servant Leadership

- Fostering a humanistic, inclusive, and diverse workplace

- Empowering autonomous teams

- Selecting and placing the right person in the right job

The "capacity for renewal" is the third organizational health function. The four leadership characteristics that support an organization's renewal capability are:

- Coaching and mentoring

- Building a learning culture

- Environmental scanning

- Lean Startup Practitioner

Nothing is surprising on the list of 13 HASIO Leadership Model characteristics. Leadership scholars have produced similar lists of leadership characteristics for their leadership models.

What is unique about the HASIO Leadership Model is that it is derived from the processes needed to realize the HASIO organizational model elements and factors to create a highly-engaged workforce in a healthy and agile organization.

Advancing the Study of Leadership in Public Organizations

According to an extensive review of 66 leadership theories, researchers concluded that "[a]s a field, we have amassed an extensive body of research and theory that has solidified the importance of leadership in organizational science."[xxiii] The researchers then argue that to advance leadership theory, linking leadership interventions to organizational outcomes is needed.

The HASIO Leadership Model links leadership effectiveness to organizational outcomes because the HASIO Organizational Model was created to design highly-effective public organizations. From my original charge to determine what makes a public agency healthy, I realized that organizational health is closely tied to organizational agility and high employee engagement.

A public agency needs good health and an engaged workforce to be agile in effectively carrying out the agency's mission and strategic goals in today's volatile, uncertain, complex, and ambiguous (VUCA) environment. The HASIO public agency needs a HASIO Leader to carry out the agency's mission.

TRANSFORMING THE GOVERNMENT HUMAN RESOURCES OFFICE (2018)

In 2017, the International Public Management Association for Human Resources (IPMA-HR) concluded an intense study of public sector human resources management. IPMA-HR performed the study because government human resource departments need to move from being transactional to transforming the agencies they serve. According to the report, "**many public HR departments lack the support, exposure, and resources to make the transition from transactional to transformational**" (p. 3). The IPMA-HR argues that if the government tries to better the lives of citizens, then government agencies need an engaged, innovative, ethical, efficient, and productive workforce.

IPMA-HR created a framework to help agencies achieve transformational public sector human resources management. The framework starts with three critical lenses: business acumen, innovation, and strategic orientation. Supporting the three lenses are five focus areas: leadership, culture, talent, communication, and technology. By working on the five focus areas, agency human resources department will improve their business acumen, increase innovation, and work more effectively with the agency's strategic mission.

The three lenses and five areas of focus work together to create a holistic framework for planning, communicating and implementing HR services that will meet the strategic and tactical needs of the organization. The framework is scalable and relevant to all sizes of HR organizations. (p. 3)

The Three Lenses

The first lens is business acumen which "is the ability to see the organization with an executive-level mentality" (p. 5). Traditionally, human resources professionals have been the "rules cops" who are only interested in the narrow enforcement of human resources policies. To become a transformational human resources department, the human resources professionals must develop a strategic view of the agency's mission and how to fashion human resources policies to help the agency fulfill its mission.

The second lens is innovation. Most organizations do not view the human resources department as an innovation leader. However, the human resource department has a "unique and comprehensive view of the organization and as such can assist in finding efficiencies and other opportunities to streamline operations and deliver services more effectively" (p. 6). The key is to develop the human resources department's business acumen and to build the strategic orientation lens.

The final lens, strategic orientation, calls for the human resources department to shift from being transactional to consultative. Strategic orientation is defined as the ability to "broadly assess the environment, develop an understanding of the challenges and opportunities facing the organization, and craft a pathway from the current state to the future state" (p. 6). The common theme of all three lenses is the ability of the human resources department to expand its perspective beyond purely human resources management concerns to the entire organization's interests. Next, the five focus areas that support the three lenses.

The Five Focus Areas

Leadership, regarding the report, means the systemic leadership approach. The human resources leader links human resources management with the broader agency strategic and mission concerns. In the last ten years, there have been many articles about human resources management gaining a seat at the senior management table. According to the IPMA-HR report, the best way to achieve that seat is to practice the three lenses.

Closely related to the leadership focus area are the two focus areas: culture and talent. For culture, the human resources department builds a positive organizational culture through three core interdependent values. First is "caring" which support the employees' well-being. The second value is "learning" which means an increased focus on employee development. The third value, "innovation," connects back to the second lens. As seen by the three culture values, there is an increased focus on valuing and developing the agency's talent. The goal of the talent focus area is to rebrand the government as the employer of choice.

"Technology is a key driver in creating potential opportunities and success as HR prepares organizations to deliver services and respond to the challenges of the future" (p. 13). The report describes several ways that technology can support the transformational capabilities of the human resources department. For example, the agency can use a human resource information system (HRIS) to deliver accurate and real-time workforce data to aid in strategic planning. Human resources departments can also use customer relationship management to understand their customers better.

The final focus area is communication. Communication is probably the most effective tool of the agency's human resources department – if used correctly. Good communication helps the human resource department build a compelling employer brand to attract new talent. Then, communication is used to increase employee engagement to help employees develop their potential. Finally, communication from agency employees on social networks helps to educate and engage citizens.

Transforming the Government Agency Starts with Transforming the Human Resources Departments

"It has been clear for some time that the Human Resources function can no longer afford to be purely transactional. Many public sector HR departments lack the support, exposure, and resources to make the transition from transactional to transformational" (p. 3). IPMA-HR's three lenses and five focus areas provide the path forward for agency human resources departments to transform themselves and their agencies.

PROCESS LITERACY: A NECESSARY SKILL FOR GOVERNMENT WORKERS OF THE FUTURE (2018)

On October 11, I was part of *Government Executive* and *NextGov's* panel on "Architecting the Future of Federal Automation." The panel was part of the three-day *Fedstival 2018* where participants explored the future of the federal government. My panel was about artificial intelligence and automation to help government agencies better deliver citizen services while improving the internal processes of government agencies. Unlike the other panels, myself and the other panel member, a government accountant, were chosen because we were not in the traditional technology roles.

What we discussed is how artificial intelligence, the blockchain, digital twins, the Internet of Things, and automation were affecting all areas of the federal agencies. For example, Mike Wetklow from the National Science Foundation described how accounting has dramatically changed with blockchain and artificial intelligence. When Mike recently visited one of his former accounting professors, he learned that accounting students today are becoming proficient in coding the programs the handle the traditional accounting tasks.

I spoke about how automation and artificial intelligence was changing the training and development of federal employees. My main point was that federal workers were transitioning from working in processes to becoming the designers and managers of automated processes. Federal workers are also using artificial intelligence to augment their decision-making skills. To understand the change in federal employees' role, we need to first distinguish between automation and artificial intelligence.

What is Automation?

Automation is the mechanical or software simulation of human actions. Think of the programs that make up the modern software office productivity tools. The word processor, the spreadsheet, and the desktop database program all can record user actions and then play back the actions as a macro. Early software macros had little or no decision-making ability. Users could program the macros at certain points to pause and wait for input from the user before proceeding to the next automated step.

More sophisticated automation programs can incorporate decision making into the recorded processes, but this requires pairing the automation program with artificial intelligence. Although automation and artificial intelligence are closely related, artificial intelligence has a profound difference over automation: the ability to learn.

What is Artificial Intelligence?

Artificial intelligence tries to simulate the process of human thinking. Modern artificial intelligence systems use methods such as neural networks and deep learning to make sense of large datasets. From the large datasets, artificial intelligence systems create rules that the system uses when confronting new sets of data.

Sometimes, artificial intelligence systems have developed new rules and processes that human intelligence would not have produced. This phenomenon is called the black box problem of artificial intelligence in which the artificial intelligence system's algorithms are not discernable to people. The black box problem can pose significant issues for government agencies because government processes must be transparent and equitable.

Process Literacy

In discussing the difference between automation and artificial intelligence, I stressed how federal employees not only need to have data-literacy but, also be process-literate. In my past career as an information technology project manager and developer, I have seen the costs of automating a poorly designed process. The bulk of my work as an information technology developer ensured that I had an optimal model of the process so the computer program would the most effective and efficient it could be.

As federal employees transition from working in processes to designing and managing processes, they need to become more effective designers of business processes. Federal workers also need to be good stewards of artificial intelligence systems because of the danger of unethical algorithms. **One reported example is Google**

Translate's sexism in translating certain words.[xxiv]

Government Jobs of the Future

Deloitte's Center for Government Insights recently released a report envisioning the **possible government of jobs in 2025**.[xxv] The report's authors see three significant shifts driving the government jobs of the future:

- Employees will be the center of the work with an emphasis on the continual development of the government employee.

- Improving the employees' decision making with artificial intelligence-powered automation systems.

- Learning in the flow of work where employees will receive training "just in time" to complete tasks.

Of particular interest is the future government job of "talent cloud coordinator." The talent cloud coordinator manages the government workforce ("the Talent Cloud") by deciding where to best deploy government employees for the maximum utilization of skills, knowledge, and abilities. The talent cloud coordinator's decisions are augmented by artificial intelligence systems while transactional tasks are handled by automated systems. The talent cloud coordinator also uses artificial intelligence systems to help in best developing government employees.

Artificial intelligence and automation have great potential to transform the government workforce. However, the greatest strength is in human talent for designing and managing the processes that run the government.

TRAINING THE NEXT GENERATION OF FEDERAL GOVERNMENT PROGRAM AND PROJECT MANAGERS (2019)

In a recent Government Executive column, John Kamensky writes about the **second anniversary of the passage of the Program Management Improvement and Accountability Act (PMIAA)**. "Two years after its passage, slow but steady progress is being made to implement not only the law's requirements but also its underlying intent—to improve the government's ability to manage large and complex programs," Kamensky writes.[xxvi]

The Office of Management and Budget has a five-year plan to implement the PMIAA. The first phase of the five-year plan was to create governance networks in the 24 major federal agencies. The second phase is conducting portfolio reviews for major acquisition programs. However, it is the third phase that most interest me – building the leadership and technical capacity to manage complex programs.

Formalizing the Program/Project Manager Role in Government

Kamensky writes:

OMB is working with the Office of Personnel Management to define the strategic talent management needs of agencies and the training needed by the current workforce. They are also working on defining potential job series, career paths, and mentoring programs, with an initial focus on acquisition staffs. OPM has announced that it will be conducting assessments next year of program and project managers across federal agencies to determine the competencies of the management workforce. According to Federal Times, this will be done in a phased approach across four groups of agencies beginning in May 2019.

I agree with Kamensky's reasons on why implementing the PMIAA is more difficult than initially thought. The first and second reasons revolve around defining what a government program is and how to manage a government program. The first two reasons probably lead to the third reason which is that many program managers do not see themselves as program managers. "They see themselves in the context of their professional communities (e.g., social worker) or their career's policy domain (e.g., managing foster care)."

I especially agree with this point.

"Furthermore, program management has traditionally been treated as an acquisition function, when in fact it is a much broader role, involving human resources, IT, financial management, mission-delivery functions, potentially other agencies, contractors, the media, and even Congress."

Program and Project Management are Similar, but the Differences are Significant

It is the third phase that will be the real challenge. The first reason is that program management and project management, although closely related, have enough significant differences that only training for program management will not address the shortage of trained project managers. The second reason is there are 15 types of government programs with wildly different characteristics and purposes (pp. 7 to 8 of **A Framework for Improving Federal Program Management**, 2018[xxvii]). Each type of program will require a diverse variety of management techniques along with a standard set of project management skills.

Even the most inclusive list of discrete skills struggles to capture the complex, imaginative, and dynamic experience of leading a federal program. Successful leaders require discrete skills, and the capacity to deploy those skills skillfully and strategically, to meet changing circumstances. Program managers themselves have a wide range of views about the skills they need, given the demands of their programs. (p. 40 of the **Framework**).

Benefits Realization Management as a Vital Skill

One set of skills that can be universally applied to all government programs and projects is benefits realization management. The purpose of benefits realization management is to determine how the program or project will deliver the benefits promised. According to the Project Management Institute (PMI), "[o]nly 61 percent of projects key to putting strategy in place yielded the intended strategic benefits" (*Strengthening Benefits Awareness in the C-Suite* (2016)).[xxviii]

Benefits realization management has been adopted by the United Kingdom in managing its government projects. The Office of Government Commerce first published a benefits realization management standard in 2007 with the latest revision being released in 2017. In the United States, benefits realization management has not caught on in the federal government. However, it is slowly being adopted in the private sector. PMI published a standard in 2016 and has a web site devoted to benefits realization management resources.

There are two advantages of incorporating benefits realization management training. The first advantage is that by communicating the expected benefits of the program or project up front, there will be more agency support and, possibly, public support for the program or project. The second advantage is that the program and project managers can replace return-on-investment (ROI) measures with the superior actual-return-on-investment (AROI). Instead of focusing on whether the program or project was delivered on time, on a budget, and within scope, the program or project is measured on the benefits achieved.

There are promising initiatives in meeting the project management and program management training challenge as PMIAA enters the next three years of implementation. Individual agencies are working hard to meet the training challenges as Kamensky recounts in his article. Training will only benefit the government by increasing the success rates of government projects.

I look forward to seeing what will happen in the next three years of PMIAA's implementation.

Transforming Government Policy Essays

FIVE EMERGING TOOLS AND METHODS FOR POLICY MAKING (2015)

Recent advances in big data and data science have revolutionized many of the scientific fields from physics to medical science. The social sciences such as economics have also seen revolutions in analysis such as behavioral economics and complexity economics. Inevitably, new analytical techniques spawned by today's data science advances would find their way into the field of policy making. In this column, five emerging analytical tools and management methods are surveyed to determine their impact on policy analysis and policy implementation.

Randomized Control Trials

Randomized control trials (RCT) are probably the most familiar analysis tool for medical and psychology researchers. It is the classic experimental design where there are a control group and a group receiving the treatment. Recently, RCTs are making their way into policy analysis because of the ability to surface unexpected findings. For example, in the story, "Reality Check," from the November 12, 2013 issue of *Wired*, Jan Kallwejt describes an RCT example. This RCT disproved the theory that giving out free textbooks to African students would increase test scores and led to the search for alternative explanations. This experience led to the "randomistas" movement in the social sciences. RCTs are now being rapidly adopted for much policy analysis.

Policy Informatics

Big Data and Data Science have made a tremendous impact on our world in areas ranging from health informatics to social networking analytics. The policy field has seen the rise of policy informatics where cutting-edge data science techniques are applied to a wide range of policy analysis and implementation issues. According to Erick Johnston in *Governance in the Information Era* (2015), "[policy informatics] appl[ies] a combination of computational thinking, complex systems modeling, data analytics, and participatory science" to help governments deal with complex governance problems. Data science adds another set of quantitative tools to the policy analysts' toolkit of statistical methods.

Process Mining

Most policy implementations involve creating at least one process. Much of policy analysis consists in examining a policy's processes to determine how to implement the policy more effectively. Process mining is an emerging management field that examines workflow data to discover how processes work and learn ways to improve processes. Process miners use data for events that occur in the process as work is passed from one process node to another. This data, which is collected into an event log, is analyzed with specialized software to map how workflows in the process. Policy analysts could create policy event logs to map how work and information flow in a policy process or even policy networks.

Design Thinking

Design thinking is a solution-based method of problem-solving. Design thinking differs from the traditional problem-oriented approach to policy analysis because design thinking focuses on iterating toward a solution that fulfills the desired outcome. Design thinkers use various methods to develop empathy with the people who will use the future solution. Stakeholders are interviewed to discover what they perceive is a problem. Design thinker practitioners then create prototypes to gain feedback from the stakeholders. The advantage of design thinking is that the almost constant input from the eventual users of the solution guarantees acceptance of that solution.

Project Management (Including Agile Project Management)

Laurent Kummer wrote in his blog on Six-Sig CMT about the parallels between policy-making and project management. In his March 8, 2015 posting, "500 Million Stakeholders,"[xxix] Mr. Kummer argues that policy making, and project management share the goal of solving a problem or introducing something new. Policy implementation and project management also involve creating a temporary organization that implements a solution with a definite start date and end date. There are also other parallels between policy implementation and project management beyond what Mr. Kummer notes. For example, the risk management techniques of project management can be applied to policy and policy implementation.

Traditional project management has much to offer policy making but so does the recent innovation of agile project management. Agile project management differs from traditional project management in that agile project practitioners iterate toward the eventual project product based on stakeholder feedback. Like design thinking, iterating toward the ultimate project product also encourages more buy-in by the stakeholders. Iterating toward a final policy solution could also be more effective than the traditional method of policymaking.

The Advantages of these New Tools and Methods

Why is there a need for new tools of policy making? The traditional tools of policy analysis still have their place, but complex policy and governance issues call for new analytical tools and implementation methods. The five tools and methods surveyed above have two advantages for policymaking. The first advantage is that RCT, policy informatics, and process mining introduces new data analysis methods to test policy assumptions better and determine causal factors for policy analysis and policy implementation. The second advantage is that design thinking and project management uses well-tested management methods to improve policy implementation. These new tools and methods add to the policy maker's toolkit.

GOVERNMENT AGENCIES NEED CITIZEN EXPERIENCE AND NOT USER EXPERIENCE (2015)

Rebooting the digital infrastructure of the federal government is one thankless task with low visibility but is vitally important. Improving the federal governement's digital infrastructure may be the most enduring legacy of President Obama's administration; if he can accomplish this Herculean task. Toward this end, the Presidential Innovation Fellows were created and now housed in the cool-sounding government startup – 18F.

18F is part of the larger U.S. Digital Service and was created through the recruiting efforts of President Obama and his Chief Technology Officer, Todd Parks. The idea is to recruit the technology stars from Google, Facebook, and the other successful West Coast technology companies to lend their expertise to Federal agencies. If it worked for Facebook then why not for the government?

Customer Service or Citizen Service?

At the heart of the successful Internet companies such as Google, Facebook, and Amazon is sales. Ninety percent of Google's revenue comes from selling ads. It is true that Google is innovative and funds many worthy projects.

Even so, Google became the company it is today because it monetized search. Google, Amazon, Facebook, and the other tech companies have perfected the art of compelling users to click and keep clicking on advertisements, games, and other money-making applications.

The 18F techies bring this customer service mindset to the Federal agencies. Having a customer service mindset is not a bad thing, and agencies can undoubtedly improve their customer service. However, the government is more than a vending machine where tax dollars go in, and services come out.

I realize that not all 18F techies have the government vending machine perspective. Some see government as a platform which enables government as "a vehicle for coordinating the collective action of citizens" (Mitch Wagner quoting technology guru Bill O'Reilly in "Government As A Platform, Not A Vending Machine," *Information Week*, August 13, 2009).[xxx]

However, do the Federal agencies see government as a platform or as a vending machine? Because of the Obama Administration directives to improve customer service, it is easier to improve the delivery of government services with a new app or a more user-friendly website. Improve the user experience (UX), and citizens might not notice that behind the easy-to-use mobile app is the same old Weberian bureaucratic process.

There is a rare opportunity to improve not just the UX for the American public but to improve the *citizen experience* (CX). Much has been written about the dangers of the disconnect between the American government and its citizens.

Could realizing government as a platform with the opportunities for citizen collaboration; agile, transparent government processes; and real-time performance reporting repair the disconnect?

Let a 1,000 Citizen Experience Startups Bloom

The U.S. Digital Service is a necessary catalyst for helping agencies to improve citizen experience and creating a government as a platform. The next step is to replicate the 18F model into the agencies. Rebooting the digital infrastructures of the agencies will take a concentrated effort with close collaborations between technology experts and the agency's subject matter experts.

There is no one government digital infrastructure but a collection of infrastructures with different architectures, capabilities, and limitations. Centralizing legacy digital infrastructures will be resource-intensive, take many years, and diverts attention from the real issue of providing a better citizen experience.

The better alternative is to work with the existing agency technologies to improve the citizen experience. Cloud technologies allow agencies to smoothly transition from building and supporting massive IT infrastructures to having their digital infrastructure supplied as a service. Moving to the cloud will relieve agencies of the burden of maintaining legacy digital infrastructures.

Then, agencies can free up resources to focus on the agency mission and improving the citizen experience. Moving to the cloud will require not only technological expertise but communication expertise, strategy expertise, and public policy expertise. All this expertise can be found in agencies now; the expertise must be coordinated and focused toward the goal of improving citizen experience.

Design Democracy

The greater lesson that government can learn from the technology startups is not how to modernize a digital infrastructure or create an app. Some government agencies already do an excellent job with their infrastructure (NASA for example) or building mobile apps (the Department of Labor and the Census Bureau are major innovators in developing apps).

What the technology experts from 18F can teach agencies is how to use design thinking and user experience concepts to develop the citizen experience field. Facebook, LinkedIn, YouTube, Amazon, and other technology companies have valuable lessons on how to use technology to encourage people to collaborate, contribute, and coordinate around a common shared purpose.

The technology companies used these user experience techniques to grow into multi-billion-dollar companies. Maybe these same techniques can also improve how government agencies operate and provide better citizen experience for the American public.

DATA ANALYTICS TO INSIGHTS LEADS TO BETTER PUBLIC ADMINISTRATION (2015)

Big Data and data analytics have been widely embraced in public administration. Many public administration programs have added more data analysis classes with some schools offering concentrations, certifications, or degrees in data science. Arizona State University has formed a policy informatics network for researchers and practitioners.

The White House, through the Evidence and Evaluation function of the Office of Management and Budget, requires agencies to create budget requests and manage programs based on rigorous data analysis. Both the Partnership for Public Service and the IBM Center for the Business of Government regularly produce publications on how to use data science to manage public agencies and programs better.

Data analytics is not new to public administration. Good policy analysis has always relied on data and statistical analysis to understand policy issues and formulate policy responses.

What has changed is the ability to collect data. Collecting data in the past could be very expensive, time-consuming, and limited to the endurance of the often human research subjects. Today, agencies have access to vast amounts of data created by the clicks and comments of millions of online users. This data deluge will soon be overwhelmed by the more massive wave of data coming from the devices connected to the Internet of Things.

The analytical tools have also become more powerful with an increase in raw computing power and the new data science techniques from Big Data researchers. Data can be crunched, sliced, diced, and visualized with point-and-click ease. There are many free open-source tools to analyze and visualize data along with even more free training resources suitable for even the most novice user.

Never has it been easier to use data to make good evidence-based decisions. What is missing that can turn all this data and analysis into something useful?

Insights are the Goal of Analytics

The Federal government collects an enormous amount of workforce data on its two-million-plus civilian employees. There is the transactional data which details who works where for how long and for what pay along with their work history, educational history, and training information. There is the annual Federal Employee Viewpoint Survey, which captures employee perceptions of their work, managers, and agency. The last seven years of my career have had me immersed in Federal workforce data to create reports and visualizations that are snapshots of the current state of the Federal civilian workforce.

Even so, what is known about the Federal workforce? There have been studies on Best Places in the Federal Government to Work, attitudes about leadership, and level of employee engagement in the agencies. Some agencies, such as the Federal Deposit Insurance Corporation (FDIC), created a program to develop trust in the work environment. The FDIC's employee engagement program was created after the insights gained from having low employee engagement scores. The insights allowed the FDIC to develop a strategy to move the agency eventually into one of the top three places to work in the Federal government. The FDIC used the data and the analysis to generate insights upon which to build a strategy around. Insights are the real value of data analytics.

Discovering Insights

Marco Vriens in his book, *The Insights Advantage* (2012), defines insights as "[t]houghts, facts, data, or analysis of facts and data that induce meaning and further understanding of a business challenge and create an urgency to act or rethink a business challenge in terms of its problems or solutions."

He explains how the proper management of insights leads to five advantages: avoiding mistakes, early warning signals, increased efficiency, growth, and competitive advantage. Vriens advocates implementing a formal insights management process to capture, retain, and disseminate insights created by the data analytics activities.

The first step is to define the problem area with the next step being to determine what is already known. Then, data analysis projects are devised with clearly specified objectives. The research from the data analysis projects is synthesized, interpreted, and reported to decision makers. To this process, Vriens adds a unique twist: the insights database.

Realizing that it is rare for the right insight to line up with the right need at the right time, Vriens suggests building a database of insights composed of three levels. The foundational level is a complete description of the insight and the methodology behind its discovery. The second level is a summary of the insight and what problem areas in which it could apply. The third level is sentence-or-two highlights reported to decision makers periodically so the decision makers know the insights and their potential value.

Government Needs Insights Management

Governments produce a fantastic amount of information and are staffed with incredible analytical talent. What is needed are defined management processes to collect, evaluate, and disseminate these insights regularly for the maximum impact on all levels of government. Not just information sharing - insight sharing.

THE ECOSYSTEM APPROACH TO OPEN GOVERNMENT DATA ACCESS PROGRAMS (2016)

The open government data movement has rapidly spread worldwide. Over 100 nations have adopted laws relating to open access to government data. The open government data movement has spread to regional and local governments and most every major city on Earth has some form of open government data access program. **According to research by McKinsey & Company,** opening access to government data is estimated to add $3 trillion a year to the global economy. The open government data movement will continue to spread to more governments.

According to a recent article in *Government Information Quarterly* ("**Planning and designing open government data programs; An ecosystem approach**"),[xxxi] governments have different approaches to creating open government data programs.

The data-oriented approach deals solely with publication policies. A step above the data-oriented approach is the program-oriented approach which lays out a governance structure with policies and strategies.

Then, there is the user-oriented approach which, as the name suggests, is based on open government data consumer needs and capabilities. The final approach is the scorecard and impact approach that considers the greater impact of open government data policies and programs.

The other approaches are driven by the government's perception of what open government data users need or desire. There may be some feedback from the users, but not a fully-developed feedback system where users can help identify what government data should be released and how it will be used.

This need for more involvement by consumers of open government data is the impetus for the ecosystem approach to open government data programs. In the next section, the advantages of the ecosystem approach will be discussed by examining the big data ecosystem of

U.S. agriculture.

An Example of a Government Open Data Ecosystem

There are three major actors in the ecosystem approach: open government data providers, open government data users, and open government data beneficiaries. The open government data providers publish data then used by open government data users (such as transparency advocates and civic technologists) to create data products. The data products are used by open government data beneficiaries such as citizens and even other governments. Feedback loops run throughout the ecosystem and help open government data providers and open government data users to release data and build data products.

In January of 2016, the **Congressional Research Service released a report**[xxxii] that mapped the big data ecosystem for U.S. agriculture. The report mapped how data flows from creators and consumers in the economic activity of U.S. agriculture. The researchers found that data flowed from government data producers and private data producers and that the data combined and recombined in complex ways.

Feedback loops were also a complex tangle of information. By mapping the data flows of this ecosystem, federal agencies can craft better policies to release and distribute open government data for the maximum benefit to open government data users and open government data beneficiaries.

A Demand-Driven Open Government Data Program at Health and Human Services

An example of the ecosystem-based approach to an open government data program is at the Department of Health and Human Services (HHS). The U.S. health care data ecosystem is arguably just as large and complex (if not more extensive and more complex) as the U.S. agriculture data ecosystem. HHS is testing the "Demand-Driven Open Data" (DDOD) program.

Instead of making a simple request for HHS data, a user describes who will use the requested data, how the requested data will be used, and the value of releasing the data. This information is compiled into a "use case." All use cases are public, and requestors are asked first to search existing use cases before making their request. Creating use cases avoids duplication of requests and helps HHS understand how and why the HHS data will be used.

HHS also encourages building communities around the datasets. As users review the requests of other users, new tools and ways of using the datasets can be created by joint efforts of the agency and open government data users. To support the communities, HHS will offer tools such as **"ontological tagging"** and **"full data dictionaries."**

A Global Ecosystem of Open Government Data?

If more governments adopted the ecosystem approach to open government data programs, would it be possible to connect these ecosystems? Mapping ecosystems would make searching for open government data easier and for combining datasets to create even newer forms of data products.

As open government data increases its impact on the world economy, it is vital that governments understand the consumers and benefits of open government data. The ecosystem-based approach seems to be the most appropriate model for governments.

NUZZLING CITIZENS AS PUBLIC POLICY: REVIEWING ROOM'S *AGILE ACTORS ON COMPLEX TERRAINS* (2016)

In 2011, Dr. Graham Room released his seminal work on applying complexity theory to public policy analysis. This book greatly influenced my work as a policy practitioner in the U.S. Federal government. Thus, I was greatly excited to see his latest book, *Agile Actors on Complex Terrains* (2016), which expands upon Room's concepts. In this review, I will explain how Room's books are connected to Room's concept of public policymaking - "nuzzling."

Agile Decision Making – The Eight Steps

In Room's previous book, *Complexity, Institutions, and Public Policy* (2011), he describes the "Agile Policy-Making Toolkit." This eight-step process aids the policymaker in constructing policy solutions for complex issues. Based on the fitness landscape concept, the agile policymaker first maps the specific policy landscape while identifying the protagonists and modeling their struggle on the landscape.

The agile policymaker attempts to civilize the struggle by looking for tipping points and energizing the protagonists. The policymaker uses various policy interventions to tune the landscape and to prevent predators from taking unfair advantage of the now civilized struggle.

In developing the agile policy-making toolkit, Room merges both complexity theory with an institutional theory to describe a method for dealing with complex policy challenges. Room does not mention the agile policy toolkit in his newest book, but you can see the influence in his two latest concepts.

Transformative Realism

In the first section of the book, Room examines how actors use micro-actions to produce changes on the macro-scale. The important point is that the macro-scale changes self-organize as in the classic example of Schelling's research on how segregated neighborhoods emerge. According to Schelling's research, if a slight majority of actors prefers neighbors just like themselves, communities will form homogenous clusters.

Room argues this research is a good start but, does not consider how institutions can block actors from creating macro-changes while empowering other actors to construct significant macro-changes.

Transformative realism is essentially Room's agile policy-making fitness landscape with its protagonists using their micro-actions to gain an advantage on the larger macro-scale of the landscape. The actors have their goals but must also contend with pre-existing institutions and the purposes of the other actors. Transformative realism sets the stage for the second section on agile actions.

Agile Actions

Room starts the second section on agile actions with this question: "[h]ow can we make sense of how social actors probe the complex and turbulent landscapes they find themselves?" He examines Popper's theories and Goldthorpe's theories on rational actions to examine how actors use their micro-actions to affect macro-scale changes.

Room states that purposive-action theories are too linear, as the theories do not account for the interactions between the actors. Actors are continually probing their environment and readjusting their micro-actions in response to other actors' micro-actions and macro-scale effects.

Room calls agile actors as "menu-makers" instead of just "menu-takers." According to Room, menu-takers choose from the existing options available to them on the macro-scale landscape. Menu-makers also act as menu-takers in that menu-makers will choose from existing options – when it suits the menu-makers purpose. When needed, the menu-maker will create new possibilities not available on the menu. What limits (or amplifies) a menu-makers ability to develop new possibilities is a significant part of Room's analysis.

The Vital Role of Institutions

Actors need a safe ground from which to create new options as they continually explore the transformative realism landscape and how their actions influence the landscape. Institutions provide that safe ground in the "settled body of habits and conventions, involving rules of thumb and standard templates."

Actors work in the tension between a "sociology of order" and a "sociology of control." Under sociology of order, institutions enforce rules guiding how actors interact with each other while providing the authority behind sanctioned choices. Here, institutions provide the menu of options from which actors can choose. In sociology of order, actors are compelled to be menu-takers.

In contrast, sociology of control allows the actors to become menu-makers. Actors can choose a "multiplicity of institutional terrains" (quoting Room) where the actors can alter the institutions to suit the actor's purposes. Institutions, Room writes, are "the connective tissue which agile social actors re-weave, as they probe and shape the transformative dynamics of their world."

Room sees institutions as the mediating mechanism in which actors can draw upon contributed mental models of the landscape. Institutions also provide the means for actors to communicate and coordinate with each other as they use their micro-actions to create macro-scale effects.

From Nudge to Nuzzle

Room ends the book by advocating "nuzzling" actors while the actors seek to reshape their landscapes. Nuzzling is beyond the concept of "nudging." Policymakers use nudges in a choice architecture to help actors make the "right choice" when choosing a policy option.

According to Room, nuzzling provides safety to the actors while giving the actors the freedom to choose the appropriate micro-actions to bring about the desired macro-affects. Nuzzling can increase citizen engagement because nuzzling involves the citizens in co-creating policy actions. As Room concludes, nuzzling can reclaim the promise of deliberative democracy.

A PROPOSAL FOR A DECADE DEVOTED TO EFFECTIVE POLICY IMPLEMENTATION RESEARCH AND PRACTICE (2017)

Between nine percent and 47 percent of jobs will be lost to artificial intelligence in the next ten years according to experts. Most of these will be low-skilled and repetitive jobs but, a significant portion could also be high-skilled and high-paying jobs such as financial planning and medical diagnosis. To put those figures in perspective, the unemployment rate during the 2008-2010 Great Recession was 10 percent while the unemployment rate during the 1930s Great Depression was 25%.

However, many economists believe that the potential job losses will be offset by new jobs created in response to increasing artificial intelligence automation. According to a pair of reports released by the White House's National Science and Technology Council's Committee of Technology, the Federal government will play a vital role in helping the American workforce move to a heavily-automated economy.

The first report, "Preparing for the Future of Artificial Intelligence,"[xxxiii] discusses the broad impact of artificial intelligence. According to the consensus of experts, artificial intelligence systems will not equal, much less exceed, the general level of human intelligence. Instead, specialized artificial intelligence will surpass human performance on many specialized tasks (such as medical diagnoses).

The second report was a follow-up to the first report. "Artificial Intelligence, Automation, and the Economy"[xxxiv] focused on preparing the American economy for five primary economic effects:

- "Positive contributions to aggregate productivity growth;

- Changes in the skills demanded by the job market, including greater demand for higher-level technical skills;

- Uneven distribution of impact, across sectors, wage levels, education levels, job types, and locations;

- Churning of the job market as some jobs disappear while others are created; and

- The loss of jobs for some workers in the short-run, and possibly longer depending on policy responses."

As the report authors admit, the magnitude of the five events is hard to determine. The economy could absorb the economic effects and mitigate the damage to the workforce. Or, the economic impacts could produce a massive shock requiring emergency government intervention such as the stimulus policies championed by President Obama when he first took office.

Other factors such as technological changes, climate change, and increasing globalization could also interact with increasing artificial intelligence automation to magnify economic disruption. Policymakers do not know the final economic impacts of increasing artificial intelligence automation.

The report suggests three broad strategies: "invest and develop artificial intelligence for its many benefits;" "educate and train Americans for jobs of the future;" and "aid workers in the transition and empower workers to ensure broadly shared growth." It is the last two strategies I will focus on because public policy academics and practitioners can play an essential role in advising the Federal government in implementing the strategies.

Lessons from Pressman's *Implementation*

A book with a profound influence on my thinking about public policy was Jeffrey Pressman's *Implementation*. Jeffery Pressman's case study of how the Economic Development Administration spent millions of dollars to convince an ever-increasing number of participants to help create employment opportunities is a classic example of the disconnect between policy goals and implementing the policy goals.

As Pressman found, the increasing number of stakeholders directly increased the number of steps in implementing a works program for Oakland, California. Along with the growing number of stakeholders and process steps, the risks of failing also increased. Even if each process step had a 95 percent chance of succeeding, the cumulative probability of success is less than 50%.

Educating and training Americans for future jobs while helping workers to transition the effects of increasing artificial intelligence automation is a much more ambitious goal than the Economic Development Administration's Oakland Project. One advantage is that public policy scholars and practitioners have learned much more about how to implement public policies since the 1960s.

Implementing national public policies to help prepare American workers to thrive in the future artificial intelligence-dominated economy can be an excellent opportunity for the public policy academic community to work with practitioners for mutual success.

The Decade of Policy Implementation Research and Practice

My modest proposal to establish 2017 to 2027 as the decade of renewed policy implementation research and practice. As governments digitally transform themselves, new program/project management methods are used, and as new technologies arise and mature, the need to effectively and efficiently implement policies strategies is never more needed than now.

Even if the impact of artificial intelligence automation is mostly negligible, implementing new workforce development policies will be a significant boon to the U.S. economy. If the shock to the American economy is as dire as some experts predict, effective policy interventions will not only help the American public; it can increase trust and confidence in the government. Effective policy-making and implementation is one area that cannot be replaced by artificial intelligence automation.

MEETING THE CHALLENGE OF GOVERNMENT MICROSERVICES (2017)

Web 2.0 technologies such as wikis and blogs emerged around the same time that then-Senator Obama was considering his run for the Presidency. President Obama's 2008 campaign harnessed the power of Web 2.0 to help him gain the White House. It was only natural that President Obama would continue to use the same Web 2.0 technologies to help him govern. As a noted technologist, Tim O'Reilly observed, Government 2.0 began in 2009 as agencies adopted social media, created data application programming interfaces (API), and held hackathons. Government 2.0 was the re-visioning of government as a platform.

Government as a Platform

According to Tim O'Reilly, Government 2.0 uses Web 2.0 collaborative technologies to help governments and citizens work together to solve problems. Government as a platform is where government convenes participants and enables citizens and third parties to create solutions from government data and services. Citizens actively co-create (sometimes leading the creation of) government services.

Government as a platform contrasts with the previous model of "vending machine government." Government as a vending machine means that the government provides a predetermined menu of services from which the citizens choose. The solutions are solely created by the government with little or no citizen participation. Vending machine government worked in the days when collaboration technologies were limited to postal mail and town halls. However, in the days of instant and deep collaboration, government as a platform has increased the effectiveness and efficiency of government services.

The Rise of Microservices

Technology platforms arose from the technology that built Google, Facebook, Twitter, and other collaborative services. Application programming interfaces (APIs) are how computer programs share data and interact with each other. For example, APIs built by the U.S.

Census Bureau allows users to find and use census data in third-party applications.

For example, a mobile app can pair Google Maps with Census data to provide demographic information about a neighborhood. There is an increasing demand for government agencies to present their data in APIs as developers realize the value of government data in building mobile applications.

Private-sector and public-sector APIs are multi-billion-dollar business in the American economy. Because of the vital economic importance of APIs, developers created microservices to mitigate the damage of failed APIs. Microservices perform only one function of the API. Each microservice is autonomous, independent, and self-contained.

The theory is that if a particular microservice fails, another microservice can quickly fill in and help the API continue to deliver data and services. Microservices work in a sort of ecosystem within the platform. If you have ever used Google Docs or watched a film on Netflix, you have used microservices.

Government Services as a collection of Microservices

You may wonder what do microservices have to do with government services? Continuing the analogy, if the U.S. Federal government is a platform and the agencies serve as APIs in that platform, then the services provided by the agencies are a collection of microservices. Viewing the Federal government through this analogy helps policymakers apply the lessons learned in creating and using microservices to design better and deliver government services.

For example, many government agencies follow Conway's Law in that the agency's organizational structure and ways of internally communicating reflect the services it provides to the public. For example, when I worked at the U.S. Office of Personnel Management, our organizational units managed the retirement services, set pay and leave policy and maintained the database of information about the civilian government workforce. These functions were further divided up into smaller organizational units down to a collection of microservices. This branching of functions into microservices led to the Inverse Conway's Law.

In the microservice world, the teams that create and manage the microservices are, like the microservices, small, isolated, and independent. Microservice teams can lead to silos and duplication of efforts which can be seen in many government agencies. Microservice teams also become increasingly specialized while becoming increasingly ignorant about their role in the organization's overall strategy and mission.

Competition for resources increases while communication between the teams plummets. Thus, the advantage of microservices is quickly erased by the organizational chaos caused by the creation of more and more microservices to handle the increasing demands for government services.

Cultivating the Government Ecosystem of Microservices

Companies like Uber have realized the advantages of using microservices by applying a gardening approach to the microservices ecosystem. Uber, Facebook, Google, and other microservice-dependent companies require that microservices meet high architectural, organizational, and operational standards. I suggest that the Federal government use the same standards and lessons learned to help reform how government services are created and delivered. Doing so will realize the benefits of government as a platform.

BLUE OCEAN THINKING – CREATING INNOVATIVE PUBLIC POLICY (2017)

I first read *Blue Ocean Strategy* when the book came out in 2005. The thesis by W. Chan Kim and Renee Mauborgne was a simple argument: instead of companies competing in established markets ("red oceans"), companies should create markets ("blue ocean"). The metaphors red ocean and blue ocean were chosen because red oceans summon up images of companies fiercely competing with each for market dominance, much like sharks fighting over a school of fish.

In contrast, blue oceans are wide open spaces where a company can build a market free of competing companies. Using various tools such as the Strategy Canvas, companies can discover unrealized opportunities and new customers while designing innovative services and products.

An early example of the blue ocean strategy was Cirque Du Soleil. Kim and Mauborgne describe how Cirque Du Soleil built a new market model that avoided the competitive traditional circus marketplace. How Cirque Du Soleil and other blue ocean companies develop new business models is described in the next two sections.

The Four Actions Framework

Kim and Mauborgne advise companies to build a Strategy Canvas in which companies determine the competitive factors in the marketplace. Then, using the Four Actions Framework, a company identifies which elements to reduce or eliminate while creating new competitive factors and raising existing elements.

For Cirque Du Soleil, the organization eliminated the traditional circus animals while raising the level of acrobatics. Cirque Du Soleil created the competitive factor of an overarching story to unite the acts into a mesmerizing performance. So, what guided Cirque Du Soleil in deciding which elements to eliminate, reduce, raise, or create?

Mapping the Buyer Experience Cycle Through the Buyer Utility Map

Companies chart the buyer experience cycle to discover new customers and develop new services and products. Kim and Mauborgne explain there are six stages in the buyer experience cycle: purchase, delivery, use, supplements, maintenance, and disposal.

Imagine the six stages as columns in a table. The rows are the Six Utility Layers: customer productivity, simplicity, convenience, risk reduction, fun and image, and environmental friendliness. The completed map will have 36 cells in which a company can place a customer pain point.

A French company, Groupe SEB, created a unique electric home French fry maker using the Buyer Utility Map. Groupe SEB found that French fry makers were dangerous because of the hot oil needed to cook the French fries. The hot oil also required inconvenient waste disposal of the used oil which also made cleaning the fryer difficult.

Groupe SEB eliminated the oil issue by creating a French fry cooker that used baking to make oil-free and healthier French fries. The blue ocean thinking tools and methods allowed Groupe SEB to leap ahead of their competitors and dominate a crowded marketplace.

What Does the Blue Ocean Strategy Have to Do with Public Policy?

The above is great for companies, but how can the Blue Ocean Strategy help public agencies. In the Epilogue to Kim and Mauborgne's latest book, *Blue Ocean Shift* (2017), the authors describe how Malaysia created a nonprofit research institute to develop blue ocean policy initiatives. First established in 2008, the Malaysia Blue Ocean Strategy Institute has hosted government summits for Malaysian public officials and selected private sector leaders. The purpose of the summits is to create economic and social blue ocean initiatives.

Kim and Mauborgne write that the blue ocean strategies and tools help government agencies successfully execute national strategies. The authors explain that blue ocean thinking helps break down government silos, reduces governmental agency turf wars, and encourages agencies to share information and resources to achieve blue ocean innovations. Blue ocean thinking also encourages innovative policy-making that would be hard to produce by conventional policy analysis methods.

One example of an innovative policy is Malaysia's Community Rehabilitation Program (CRP). The CRP was created to rehabilitate petty criminals. Before the CRP, the traditional government policy was to incarcerate prisoners in large prisons while severely limiting contact between the prisoners and their families.

CRP housed prisoners in spare space on military facilities and allowed for extensive contact between the prisoners and their families. Recidivism has decreased while CRP centers are 85% cheaper to build and 58% cheaper to run. The Malaysian government estimates that CRP will save taxpayers $1 billion (US dollars) in its first ten years.

Blue Ocean Policy Analysis and Making

The lessons from Malaysia's experiments with blue ocean thinking demonstrates the great value of Kim and Mauborgne's ideas. What I especially like are the two tools: The Buyer Utility Map and the Four Factor Model. Think of the citizen journey and which factors matter most to citizens. Thinking blue ocean helps to create innovative policy ideas that go beyond the tired red ocean government policies.

THE GOVERNMENT IN THE POST-CORPORATE AGE (2018)

Most governments deal with the economy either directly or indirectly. The federal government sets regulations on commercial speech, how stocks are traded, and enforce equal employment laws among a multitude of other policy actions involving the national economy. State governments oversee the creation of corporations and, through tax incentives, make the local state economies "business-friendly." Much of the history of American public administration deals with the interplay of business actions and the corresponding government reactions.

As business became big in the United States, the U.S. government became big. From the trust-busting of the Teddy Roosevelt Presidency to the creation of regulatory agencies of the Nixon Administration, government agencies handle the perceived harms and excesses of corporations. Probably the most illustrative example is the rapid growth of the regulatory state during Franklin Roosevelt's New Deal. During the 2008 Recession, the federal government stepped in to rescue those corporations that were "too big to fail."

However, what happens to the government when the business corporation is no longer the dominant player in the nation's economy? According to Gerald F. Davis, big corporations are fast declining in favor of new economic entities composed of small groups (or even individuals) who use the latest Internet technologies to build private companies. With technology platforms, open-source software, and rentable factories, entrepreneurs can make economic entities that can compete with the biggest corporations without having a large staff or the need for significant capital investments.

The Vanishing American Corporation (by Gerald F. Davis)

Gerald F. Davis chronicles the rise and fall of the American corporation in his latest book. Davis argues that corporations helped build the middle class by offering lifetime employment, health insurance, and retirement plans. Corporations also made it easier for the government to regulate the economy by being part of the public stock exchange. Reporting requirements made the internal operations of corporations at least partially transparent to the general public.

It is with the rise of Internet-based companies that corporations lost their power over the American economy. Companies like Apple, Google, Facebook, and Amazon employ fewer people but have more revenue and market power than established companies such as auto companies or General Electric. Companies like Uber have transformed the jobs economy into the gig economy made up of independent contractors who perform low-paid tasks with no benefits and possibility of long-term employment.

Capitalism without Capital: The Rise of the Intangible Economy (by Jonathan Haskel and Stian Westlake)

At the same time that the big corporation is in decline, the intangible economy is rising. Intangible assets are things like design, branding, and other intellectual property assets. Companies are not spending as much on tangible assets because, nowadays, the competitive advantage is in the business model, brand, or intellectual property possessed by the company.

Haskel and Westlake argue that the intangible economy causes economic inequality and stagnating productivity. Economic inequality and declining productivity happen because intangible assets favor highly-educated people who can create intellectual property assets and companies that can use the intellectual property infrastructure to their advantage.

Governments developed in an economy dominated by the tangible. You can see this in the tax code – especially with the property tax and recording structures of state and local governments. According to Haskel and Westlake's analysis, intangibles have four characteristics that tangibles do not. First, intangibles are scalable so the intangible asset can be copied with perfect fidelity and with little or even no cost. Second, intangible assets are sunk costs and hard to resell. For example, the processes used by Starbucks to operate their stores are unique to Starbucks and could not easily be sold.

Third, intangible assets have high spillovers so other companies can take advantage of the intangible assets that other companies create. For example, Netflix takes advantage of the Amazon network structure with many other high-tech companies. Fourth, intangibles create synergies by combining intangible assets to create more value than the simple combination of assets.

As the Economy Shifts, How Will Government Policy Shift?

Government policy usually lags behind changes in the economy. The American economy is rapidly changing from two foundational concepts that shaped much of government regulation and policy – corporations and tangible property. Corporations will still be part of the economy but, as new economic structures arise, corporations will play an even smaller role in the marketplace.

Also, government tax policies are built around the characteristics of tangible property. As intangibles play an even more significant role in the formation of the new economic structures, tax policy must grapple with the four characteristics of intangibles.

The question is if government policymakers can successfully forecast the changes wrought by the decline of corporations and the rise of intangibles. Not to stop the inevitability of these two trends but to smooth the transition from our current economy to the new future economy.

WHERE WILL GOVERNMENT BE IN THE NEXT TWENTY YEARS? (2018)

Some recent reports have had me thinking about the transformation of local, state, and the federal government in the United States. In February, I had written about the International Public Management Association for Human Resources' (IPMA-HR) **2017 report on reinventing the government human resources office**. Over two months later, two new reports mention transforming the government HR function as part of the broader strategy of changing government for the digital future.

The 2018 President's Management Agenda

Released in March, the *President's Management Agenda* sets out the goals for reforming government during the Trump administration. There are eleven "Priority Areas for Transformation" that range from "improving customer experience with federal services" to "improv[ing] transfer of federally-funded technologies from lab-to-market." There are three "key drivers of transformation" to achieve success in the eleven priority areas. The first two key drivers are technology-based ("IT Modernization" and "Data, Accountability, and Transparency") while the third driver concentrates on improving the federal workforce.

The report focuses on the third driver by displaying the "Strategic Workforce Management" model on page 19. The first part of the model is about improved employee performance management and engagement. The second part of the model advocates reskilling and redeploying human capital resources while the third part promises to implement hiring reform. Underneath the three parts are "continuous learning" through "innovation, research, and pilot projects."

The State Policy Road Map

Deloitte's Center for Government Insights released the *State Policy Road Map* in February 2018. The *State Policy Road Map* is a rich report that ambitiously attempts to chart the future for state governments. The report is divided into four sections: "Government Reform," "Delivering Essential Services," "Future State," and "Improving

Quality of Life." Like the *President's Management Agenda*, the critical drivers for transformation involve incorporating new digital technologies and artificial intelligence automation with improving the state government workforce.

In the section of the report describing how to modernize the state workforce, the authors argue that it is not the public workers at fault. Instead, the problem is in the systems that recruit, hire, train, develop, and assist the state workers. Not surprisingly, the public sector lags behind the private sector in human resources (HR) practices and technology.

What is surprising is how much the public-sector lags behind in modern HR practices and technology; especially for most states. Some of the improvement suggestions from Deloitte are to implement their "**govcloud**" concept, develop a digital HR platform to "enhance the employee's experience," and use digital workflows to augment the work experience.

2018 Global Human Capital Trends

Although this third report is not geared specifically to the public sector (although some public sector organizations were included in 11,070 executives surveyed), the *Deloitte 2018 Global Human Capital Trends* are a great set of indicators of where HR technologies and practices are going. The overall conclusion from the report is the rise of the "social organization."

Social organizations are essentially organizations in which profit is balanced with being a good corporate citizen. Internally, social organizations promote a high-level of collaboration among business units while increasing the empowerment of employees. The evolution of the social organization can be seen in the list of the ten trends:

- Teams are leading teams up and down the organization.

- The workforce ecosystem of employees, contractors, freelancers, and other alternative-arrangement workers.

- Personalized, agile, and holistic rewards systems.

- New career pathways that transition from the career model to "experiences."

- Working with older workers while incorporating millennials and Generation Z workers.

- Increasing corporate efforts to have positive social impacts.

- Focusing more on employees' well-being programs.

- Dramatically increasing the use of artificial intelligence, robotics, and automation in the workplace.

- The rise of the hyper-connected workplace.

- The ethical challenges of workforce analytics.

So, Where Is Government Going In The Next Twenty Years

Various people such as Abraham Lincoln and Peter Drucker have been attributed as the author of the quote, **"the best way to predict the future is to create it."** No matter who said it, the idea is a valid method for dealing with future uncertainty.

As the three reports demonstrate, current and future advances in technology will have profound impacts on society, the workplace, and government. The debate is still ongoing over whether artificial intelligence, robotics, and automation will doom millions of workers to unemployment or open up new opportunities beyond today's routine and unfulfilling low-wage jobs. These technologies are being rapidly assimilated into the workplace.

The challenge for government HR is recruiting, hire, train, and develop a public sector workforce that can meet the challenges of the new societal realities and work effectively in government agencies that will have changed significantly twenty years from now.

AMERICANS WANT BIG – BUT UNSPECIFIED - CHANGES IN THE FEDERAL GOVERNMENT'S DESIGN AND STRUCTURE (2018)

The Pew Research Center recently surveyed how the American public perceived America's political system and democracy in general Between January 29 and February 13, 2018, 4,656 adults were surveyed online. Then, from March 7 through 14, 2018, an additional 1,466 adults were interviewed by phone. Questions asked included how Americans felt about democratic ideals and how well the current political system upheld democratic values.

"[M]ost Americans say democracy is working well in the United States – though relatively few say it is working very well. At the same time, there is broad support for making sweeping changes to the political system: 61% say 'significant changes' are needed in the fundamental 'design and structure' of the American government to make it work for current times."[xxxv]

However, there is little agreement on exactly how the government should change. The survey focuses more on the political aspects of the American federal government such as increasing the power of the Presidency and how fairly the Congressional districts are drawn. There is agreement among both Republicans and Democrats that government is insufficiently transparent and open (73% of Democrats and 65% of Republicans). Sixty-eight percent of Democrats agree that the government needs significant changes while only 50% of Republicans believe government needs reform.

State and Local Governments Are Considered More Favorably Than the Federal Government

Except for two years after the 9/11 terrorist attacks, the federal government has lagged behind state and local government in favorability by the American public. Local government has consistently rated between the high 60s and low 70s while the state government has ranged between the upper 50s and upper 60s in the positive perceptions of American citizens. Meanwhile, the federal government usually scores between the mid-40s to mid-30s in positive ratings.

Are State and Local Governments Better Managed Than the Federal Government?

According to Don Kettl (public policy professor at the University of Maryland), "[t]he basic argument for state efficiency is based more on hopes and prayers than on clear evidence, across the board."xxxvi Because state and local governments have different programs and missions as compared to the federal government, it is difficult to compare effectiveness among the governments.

Also, state and local governments often manage portions of federal programs using federal funding which makes determining results even harder. It would be illuminating if the Pew Survey asked more about citizens' perceptions of the levels of government.

What Else Do the American People Perceive About Government's Design and Structure?

A few other hints about how to redesign government comes from four questions in the Pew Survey. The first question asks about the balance of power between the federal government's branches. Fifty-five percent of the respondents believed that the power balance between the executive, legislative, and judicial branches keeps the branches in check. Again, it would be interesting to delve further into how the 45% perceived a power imbalance between the three branches.

The second question asks if "government policies reflect [the] views of most Americans." Sixty-three percent agree that government policies do **NOT** reflect the views of the American majority. Sixty-nine percent answered the third question by agreeing that the federal government is **NOT** open and transparent. Finally, the fourth question asks if the "rights and freedoms of all people are respected" to which there was a close split: 47% agree that all rights are respected while 52% do **NOT** agree.

The above results suggest that redesigning the federal government start by making government more open and transparent while implementing policies that better reflect the views of the American majority. It will be a delicate balancing act to implement policies that respect all rights and freedoms while meeting the needs of the majority.

The Pew Survey asked about the respondent's knowledge of basic civics. "Public knowledge on civic and political questions varies widely by issue. Large majorities are familiar with the First Amendment and the role of the Electoral College, but the public struggles when asked about other topics such as the filibuster and tie-breaking procedures in the Senate." According to the survey results, there was no significant difference in civics knowledge along party lines.

Reinventing the Federal Government

The Pew Survey raises intriguing ideas about what the American people want from their federal government. First, it is readily apparent that the citizens want a more open and transparent government that better reflects the priorities of the majority. Second, Americans want the stronger protection of rights and freedoms for all Americans. Third, the checks and balances of the federal structure are maintained and strengthened. Finally, understanding why citizens hold state and local government in higher regard may help in increasing the positive perceptions of the federal government.

SHOULD POLICY RESEARCH INCREASE THE USE OF EXPERIMENTAL RESEARCH? (2018)

The successful emergence of behavioral economics can be traced to using experiments in testing fundamental economic assumptions and concepts. The most famous example of how experimenters created behavioral economics is through the ultimatum game. The rules of the ultimatum game are simple. One participant is given an amount of money to split with a second experiment participant. According to the neoclassical economic theory of the rational economic person, the second participant should accept even the most one-sided splitting of the money.

However, in numerous iterations of the ultimatum game among different cultures, researchers found that the different cultures had a fairness level. Many participants would refuse the split if they felt that the division was unfair. The findings of this experiment and similar economic games demonstrated that the original economic principle of the rational person to be expanded. A new field of economics was born out of experimentation.

The History of Experimentation in Policy Research

Huitema, Jordan, Munaretto, and Hilden (2018) write in a recent editorial note in about the use of experimentation in policy research.[xxxvii] As the authors explain, policy research has a long history of using experimentation as a research method.

Experimentation was a fundamental concept of pragmatism and championed by both Charles Peirce and John Dewey. Peirce advocated experimentation as a method of scientific research while Dewey saw experimentation as an approach to governance.

These two perspectives evolved into two variants. The first is "Darwinian experimentalism" in which many approaches are tried. The second variant is "generative experimentalism," focuses on one specific innovation and iteratively improves on the innovation through experiments.

Then, there is the influence of Donald T. Campbell. He promoted experimentation, especially randomized experiments, as the defining standard for research. Campbell created the concept of the "experimenting society" with these characteristics (from Huitema et al.'s (2018) editorial note):

- "A preference for decentralization and diversity."

- "An inclination towards action rather than inaction."

- "A premium on honest assessment based on transparent data produced in an accountable manner."

- "Willingness to change theories and values in the face of disconfirming evidence."

Despite this history, experimental studies are rare in the policy research field and mostly confined to social policy and education. When experimentation is used in policy research, it is often the Peirce view of experimentation as classical science research. Critics of experimentation argue that experiments can stifle intellectual progress because experiments focus "exclusively on means and not goals" and experiments "use significant time and resources" while focusing on "one idea at a time."

The Four Questions of Modern Policy Experiments

Huitema et al. (2018) describe four questions about experimentation in research:

- Experiments shape the reality of the system being studied by the effect that the intervention has on the system. There is "scientific reality making" which affects what is learned from the experiment and there is "political reality making" which affects the political environment around the experimental intervention.

- Policy experiments are inherently political in that the "starting premises of an experiment are often highly consequential." The choice of an experimental intervention determines which political viewpoint and political actors will prevail in the specific policy area under study.

- How the policy experiment is governed is also influenced by the choices such as the "type of information that is regarded or ignored, the authority to make decisions on the experiment, the costs, and benefits associated with the experiment." Governance decisions also play in the reality-making function and political impacts of the policy experiment.

- The final question concerns how the lessons learned from the experiment are received by policymakers and other stakeholders. Policymakers are more likely to accept experimental results that are salient, credible, and legitimate. In the long term, "experiments are likely to play a role in the gradual sedimentation of ideas in policymaking." However, the acceptance of the experimental results increases when the results align with pre-existing policy goals.

The Potential and Challenges of Policy Experiments

Policy experiments have great potential as evidenced by the groundbreaking results of experiments in other social science fields. Also, experimentation has a long tradition in policy research. What stands in the way, according to Huitema et al. (2018), is "conceptual precision" – an explicit definition of a policy experiment.

Researchers also must know of the "political dynamics surrounding and within experiments" and the governance of policy experiments. Finally, it remains "unclear which factors determine whether certain experiments lead to learning and policy change." The authors argue that policy experiments should be more than just a research method but may have a greater impact as a "broader approach to governing."

COMMUNICATION CONSTITUTES PUBLIC ORGANIZATIONS? COMMUNICATION'S ROLE IN PUBLIC ADMINISTRATION (2019)

Around the early 1980s, communication theory transitioned from the "information transmission" paradigm to the **"linguistic turn."**[xxxviii] In organizational communication, the "communicative constitution of organization" (CCO) perspective arose to explain how **organizations continually reinvent themselves through communication.**[xxxix]

CCO scholars argue that organizations are created as members use language and texts to co-create the organization's social reality. Using the CCO perspective, scholars and practitioners can understand how organizations are formed, why organizations behave in certain ways, and how the organization will evolve.

CCO is a relatively new field and still has many questions such as exactly how communication constitutes organization and the mechanisms that members use to create a shared organizational reality. However, the CCO perspective can be a fruitful area for public administration research.

Some public administration research uses the CCO perspective. For example, one article argues that better civic engagement can be achieved **by improving the internal communication channels of an agency.**[xl] However, there needs to be more public administration research using the CCO perspective – especially as CCO research is evolving rapidly. I suggest the following three research areas which can benefit from the CCO perspective.

"Elmore's Problem" of Dual Dynamics in Public Policy

In 1979, Dr. Elmore formulated his dual dynamics theory of how decisions are made in the U.S. administrative state. Congress and the Executive Branch set and react to the public policy agenda which results in a flow of information down to the governmental agencies. The priorities and goals are set for the agencies. At the same time, expertise and detailed information about specific policy issues are flowing up from the agencies which influence Congress' and

Executive Branch's attention and bargaining over the policy agenda.

Samuel Workman used the Elmore Problem to guide his research in how Congress and the federal agencies process their communications to solve policy problems. Dr. Workman's research is valuable and can benefit from the CCO perspective as Congress and the federal agencies co-create a shared reality around the policy agenda.

The Coordinated Management of Meaning in Internal and External Communications by Federal Agencies

The Coordinated Management of Meaning (CMM) arose separately from CCO, but both theories share much in common. Developed by Pearce and Cronen around the mid-70s, CMM has more acceptance among practitioners than academic scholars.

Even so, both CMM and CCO are concerned with how communication helps people to develop a shared reality. Combining the tools of CMM with the theoretical foundations of CCO can aid public administration scholars in developing research with practical application in helping agencies to improve their internal and external communications.

Government by Ventriloquism

Francois Cooren proposed his "ventriloquism" variant of CCO to describe how people bring texts and abstract concepts into co-creating the organization's social reality. Dr. Cooren explains that communicators frequently make other beings say or do things through the communicator's speech acts.

For example, when I was at the U.S. Department of Agriculture, managers would often claim to speak for the "rural population" or the "American rural community." Federal workers in the Defense agencies often justify their decisions because this is what the "warfighter" wants. "The American people" is the stock phrase of all Congressional members.

Ventriloquism also occurs when public administrators claim to speak for policy, law, regulation, or the Constitution. Thus, texts and abstract concepts become embodied in the social reality of the agency.

Taking the CCO perspective in investigating policy decisions can help the researcher better understand how policies were interpreted and implemented. The ventriloquism variant of CCO can also better illuminate the communication dynamics between Congress, the Executive Branch, and the administrative agencies.

The CCO Perspective of Public Policy and Administration

Taylor (1993) writes in Rethinking the theory of organizational communication: How to read an organization:"

I have never been able to figure out how there could be an organization in the absence of communication, existing before communication, and on a material plane distinct from it. It seems self-evident to me that organization is a **product** *[italics in original] of communication, and dependent on symbolic sense-making through interaction for its mere existence.* (p. ix).

In reviewing the public administration research literature, most scholars recognize and appreciate the role of communication in public policy and the management of public agencies. My purpose in this article is to advocate using another research perspective to understand better how public policy is formed and implemented through communication.

CCO is growing as more practitioners from around the world explore the concepts and new applications of CCO. Incorporating the latest developments of CCO into public administration research can help increase our understanding of how public administration creates and manages public policy.

Miscellaneous Essays on Public Administration

2011 – THE START OF THE COMPLEXITY ECONOMICS DECADE

As the first decade of the 21st Century ends, I hope that the economic events of the last thirty-five years finally loosen the hold that neoclassical economics has on public policy. It is widely recognized that the accepted economic models that governments use to shape policy are just not empirically valid.[xli]

Today's economies differ vastly from the industrial revolution economies that formed neoclassical economic theory. These theories are the basis for setting interest rates, regulating the stock market, determining the level of environmental protection, almost every aspect of government regulation (Smith 2010, p. 65). It is time to modernize the economic theories used to guide government and economic policies.

The case against neoclassical economics has been growing in recent years. As Yves Smith (2010) details in her book:

1) Economics is not real science because it is difficult to do the empirical evidence to validate the models economist develop from their assumptions (pp. 20-21).

2) Many of the core assumptions of neoclassicism (people are rational, have complete information, only act to maximize utility, etc.) have been disproved by experiments in behavioral economics (pp. 94-97).

3) Even though they are working with faulty assumptions, economists claim that the implications derived from the assumptions are still valid because they are good approximations of reality (p. 41 and pp. 47-48).

4) Hard sciences also use simplified models to explain phenomena, but the crucial difference is that economists add unrealistic properties to validate their models. For example, economists add the property of perfect information to make supply and demand models work (pp. 48-49).

Some economists counter by admitting that neoclassical economics has these problems, but the cure is to do more empirical research. But with more empirical research, the neoclassical assumptions are giving way to a new economic theory – complexity economics.

Eric Beinhocker (2007) surveys the rise of complexity economics in which researchers apply complexity and network theory concepts to economic activities. The main advantage of complexity economics is that its assumptions can be empirically validated and that its findings apply to modern economic phenomena. Thus, this is a better basis upon which to base policy decisions.

Beinhocker's (2007) core argument is easy to understand. Businesses use a mixture (business plan) of physical technologies and social technologies to compete with other businesses. The businesses that have more fit business plans out-compete businesses with less-fit business plans. Based on this model, Beinhocker details several implications for policymakers:

1)   The role of markets is to process the immense amount of information from buyers and sellers into the most coordinated and effective manner while also determining how fit a business is. Thus free and open markets must be maintained by regulations that do not impede the flow of information available to all parties (p. 423).

2)   Government's role is to provide and preserve the vast array of social technologies that make it possible for businesses and markets to exist. Social technologies such as contract law, antitrust enforcement, and securities regulation (p. 425). Therefore, the government plays an essential role in shaping the fitness determination role of markets (pp. 426-427).

3)   Behavioral economics indicates what kind of social programs will be more readily accepted and politically-supported. People will support aid programs that have strong reciprocity – programs designed to help people become functionally independent (pp. 418-421).

4)   Countries that score higher on measures of societal trust also have higher economic performance than countries with lower societal

trust scores (pp. 432-433). Thus, an essential role for the American government is to build up social capital in the U.S. (pp. 439-440).

As the above demonstrates, the government has a vital role in preserving and strengthening the U.S. economy. The argument of neoclassical economics that government should have little or no role in market economies is a false one and has led to extreme reactions from the Left and the Right.

With a clearer understanding of government's actual role in the U.S. economy, policymakers can craft effective policies that preserve the best features of the market system while building up the necessary social capital to strengthen the economy and serve the U.S. people. We need to move beyond the false answers given by neoclassical economics to the insights of complexity economics.

References

Beinhocker, E.D. (2007). *The origin of wealth: The radical remaking of economics and what it means for business and society.* Boston, MA: Harvard Business Press.

Smith, Y. (2010). *Econned: How unenlightened self-interest undermined democracy and corrupted capitalism.* New York: Palgrave MacMillan.

Further Reading:

Berreby, D. (2005). *Us & Them: The science of identity.* Chicago: The University of Chicago Press.

Cassidy, J. (2009). *How markets fail: The logic of economic calamities.* New York: Farrar, Straus, and Giroux.

Lehrer, J. (2009). *How we decide.* Boston: Houghton Mifflin Harcourt

Pfaff, D.W. (2007). *The neuroscience of fair play: Why we usually follow the golden rule.* New York: Dana Press.

Schelling, T.C. (2006). *Micromotives and macrobehaviors.* New York: W.W. Norton & Company.

Shermer, M. (2008). *The mind of the market: Compassionate apes, competitive humans, and other tales from evolutionary economics.* New York: Times Books.

Stiglitz, J.E. (2010). *Freefall: America, free markets, and the sinking of the world economy.* New York: W.W. Norton & Company.

Thaler, R.H., & Sunstein, C.R. (2009). *Nudge: Improving decisions about health, wealth, and happiness.* New York: Penguin Books.

Ubel, P.A. (2009). *Free-market madness: Why human nature is at odds with economics – and why it matters.* Boston, MA: Harvard Business Press.

(Originally appeared in *GovLoop*)

REINVENTING AMERICAN CITIES WITH THE CITY WEB (2016)

The President's Council of Advisors on Science and Technology (PCAST) recently released a report on strategies that use infrastructure improvements and new technologies to improve America's cities. PCAST recommends using the National Science and Technology Council to coordinate research and development activities designed to help cities increase energy efficiency, implement renewable energy technologies, and enhance connectivity among traffic systems, water management, and industrial facilities.

As the **PCAST report** points out, "Transforming cities around the world . . . is already a race – one that the United States cannot afford to lose." At the core of PCAST's recommendations is a platform to facilitate information-sharing and collaborative development: "The City Web."

Why Cities Need to Transform

Since 2011, there has been a movement back to the cities which have reversed 90 years of hollowing out American cities. The Obama administration, recognizing these demographic trends, launched the Smart Cities initiative in September 2015.

The Smart Cities Initiative coordinated pre-existing efforts by the Department of Commerce, Department of Transportation, and several other agencies along with launching the MetroLab Network. The MetroLab Network helps city governments to partner with local university research labs to help cities find innovative solutions.

There are two significant areas of focus with the Smart Cities efforts. The first area of focus is on using innovative technologies to revitalize infrastructure. The second area of focus is using the emerging technologies of embedded sensors, the Internet of Things, and big data to increase connectivity and use analytics to improve decision making.

Because changing a city's infrastructure and building connectivity can be costly and disruptive, the PCAST report recommends a new approach that allows for maximum learning and sharing of best practices among large cities and small cities.

Reinventing the City One District at a Time

According to PCAST, a district is "an area and population that are large enough for new technology implementations to have an impact, but also manageable from the point of view of clarity of intervention, tuning, collection of data, and assessment of progress and lessons learned." Using districts as experimental pilots take a lean startup approach to rebuild cities.

As I have written before, **governments can learn much from using the lean startup methodology.** Lean startup methodology is especially useful in this case because it is effective in handling complex projects with interconnected technologies and goals. Lean startup methodology also relies heavily on user input which can help build favorable citizen engagement in the district pilots.

The Need for City Web

A major theme throughout the PCAST report is the need for coordination and collaboration. There have been and still, are projects to revitalize cities. However, past improvements have been hard to replicate because of "idiosyncratic implementation, uneven distribution of solutions, and expensive implementations."

These improvements rarely produce software useful for other cities, especially smaller cities. There is no shared "app store" for civic applications and few existing networks to share innovations between civic innovators. However, the PCAST authors argue that now is the time to create a shared platform for civic innovators to share knowledge and data.

Now is the time for City Web because of five factors. First, the rise of technology-savvy civic innovation stakeholders. Second, new practices and standards for creating, storing, retrieving, and archiving digital data. The third and fourth factors are closely related because the increasing growth of Application Programming Interfaces (APIs) makes sharing digital data easier and, thus, providing for more sophisticated real-time analytics. The fifth and final factor is the use of "integrated modeling and scenario evaluation to support policy and planning." These five factors can be combined to produce a civic innovation platform that will host app stores, communities of practice, online learning, analytics products, and other support functions for civic innovators.

Four Recommendations for a Federal Government and Civic Innovators Partnership

The PCAST report concludes with four recommendations. The first recommendation advises the Department of Commerce (DoC), the Department of Transportation (DoT, Housing and Urban Development (HUD), and the Department of Energy (DoE) to form the Cities Innovation Technology Investment Initiative (CITII).

In the second recommendation, HUD will increase efforts to use technological innovation to aid low-income communities. The third recommendation advocates the establishment of two programs to support developing Urban Development Districts and to introduce new technologies into communities.

The final recommendation instructs the National Science and Technology Council (NSTC) to create the Urban Science Technology Initiative (USTI) Subcommittee. USTI will coordinate Federal research and development projects for civic innovation.

Revitalizing American Cities are becoming more vital to the American economy and society as urbanization rapidly increases. There are many challenges in reinventing cities due to decades-old (and sometimes, centuries-old) infrastructure that can be met with new sustainable, renewable technologies and data science.

HELPING PRESIDENTIAL ADMINISTRATION TRANSITIONS MAKE BETTER DECISIONS (2017)

President Obama recently signed into law a bill to improve the process of presidential transitions. This law, the Presidential Transition Improvements Act of 2015, builds on the initiatives during President Bush and President Obama transition in 2008 to 2009. Because of the urgency of the war on Terror and the 2008 Recession, it was vital to have the incoming Obama administration ready to govern from day one.

To further support future presidential transitions, the non-partisan Partnership for Public Service ("Partnership") has created the Center for Presidential Transition. The mission of the Center is to prepare a "management roadmap" for officials of the incoming administration.

Advising Government Officials on Making Better Decisions

As part of the management roadmap, the Partnership with the IBM Center for the Business of Government ("Center") released "Enhancing the Government's Decision-Making: Helping Leaders Make Smart and Timely Decisions." The report addresses effective decision making for executive leaders in the White House and the federal agencies.

It is well known to public administration scholars and practitioners that governments today face overwhelming information and analysis demands as public officials manage current programs and launch new initiatives. More data is being produced at an ever-increasing rate and complexity while decisions need to be made faster and with a more critical impact on the American public and the rest of the world.

Building an Enterprise Approach to Decision Making

The Partnership and the Center held a roundtable in November 2015 to discuss these four key areas:

1. "Establishing decision frameworks and associated governance structures."

2. "Harnessing effective governmental decision processes."

3. "Adapting decision support systems to better inform decision-making."

4. "Developing ideas and tools to enable leaders to make practical decisions in the complex federal environment."

From the roundtable discussion, the participants arrived at three recommendations. First, leaders will establish how decisions will be made for different situations. The leaders will also explain their information needs for different decision situations. Second, leaders are advised to take an "enterprise" approach to decision making.

The Partnership has written several studies on the enterprise approach to governance, so decision-makers adopt a holistic perspective in managing his or her federal agency. Third, leaders are encouraged to utilize existing support functions such as strategic foresight and enterprise risk management. In the next three sections, each recommendation will be explained.

Recommendation One – How Decisions Will Be Made

The first step in recommendation one is to determine a "unit of analysis." A unit of analysis is defined as how "[l]eaders . . . articulate how they view the world and how it works from their perspective. . . . It could be an agency, a function, a program, or an enterprise-wide approach (such as an end result or organizing around a customer)."

Once the unit of analysis is established, the decision maker needs to delineate clear links between mission, goals, and objectives. The decision maker then develops the relationships between organizational units to the mission, goals, and objectives. These three steps establish decision frameworks.

Recommendation Two – The Enterprise Approach to Decision Making

The Partnership and the Center noted that in the last decade, ad hoc governmental-wide collaborative networks have arisen to work on various policy issues. As an example, the report discusses the enterprise approach used to implement the American Recovery and Reinvestment Act of 2009 successfully. The report encourages using more cross-agency collaborations and partnerships to achieve more decisions.

To help support these decisions, the President's Management Council is encouraged to develop an enterprise governance framework while agencies with similar policy areas are advised to create a "central data analytics capacity that connects data silos used by decision-makers."

Recommendation Three – Using Foresight and Organizational Resilience to Support Better Decision-Making

Agency leaders are encouraged to strengthen or establish the decision-support functions of foresight, risk management, and institutional resilience. Foresight is essential in helping determine and prioritize decisions while risk management helps the decision makers determine the best decision outcomes.

Institutional resilience is necessary for agencies to weather the risks and unknowns in implementing decisions. Equally important is that future agency leader needs to understand fully the legal authorities, precedents, constraints that surround the decision-making environment.

Opportunities for Public Administration Scholars in Government Decision Making

The Partnership has created a rich research opportunity for public administration scholars in determining what makes effective governmental decision-making. I discussed one possible approach in my December 2015 *PATimes* column ("Rethinking Strategy for Public Agencies"). I described the central message of Lusk and Birks' *Rethinking Public Strategy,* which advocates helping agencies to develop future-thinking capabilities by using scenario planning.

There are other areas of decision-making research that can advise future government leaders to make better decisions and manage government programs.

THE DISTRIBUTED CONSENSUS TECHNOLOGY ROAD TO DIRECT DEMOCRACY? (2017)

By now, you have probably heard of the new Internet technology, blockchain. The blockchain is the technology behind Bitcoin which started the digital cryptocurrencies. Blockchain allows for a secure and decentralized way to record and verify transactions. Unlike traditional transaction systems, a central authority need not provide proof of the deals.

For example, think of the role that banks play in our economic environment. We deposit cash into the bank by using accounts to store information about how much cash we own at a given time. We can write checks or use debit/credit cards to withdraw cash. The bank verifies that we have enough cash to honor the check or debit/credit card transaction.

The bank is the central authority around which we and the people or organizations we interact with to record and verify cash transactions. We and the people or organizations we deal with depend wholly upon the accuracy and security of the account records kept by the bank.

Blockchain

Where distributed consensus technologies, such as blockchain differ, is there is no central authority to verify and secure the record of transactions. Instead, the authority is distributed among the participants in the network. Every time there is a transaction, copies of the transactions record are sent to the network participants. Then, whenever a transaction must be verified, the network is polled to confirm that most transactions record copies agree on the deal.

The distributed verification method is how **blockchain technologies work**. Blockchain has been called the "new Internet" and governments all around the world have studied using blockchain in delivering public services. However, as with all technologies, blockchain has inspired several alternatives.

Hashgraph

Hashgraph is built as an alternative to the blockchain. According to Swirlds, the licensing company, Hashgraph is built on the concept of "virtual voting." As Hashgraph members create a transaction, knowledge of the transaction is spread throughout the community within minutes.

One difference between blockchain and Hashgraph is that transactions are much faster on Hashgraph because only the effects of the transaction must be recorded. Blockchain requires consulting the old blocks for verification.

Another difference is that Hashgraph uses "virtual voting" in which the nodes can predict how each node will vote on a particular transaction because each node knows "what each node knows, and when they knew it." Virtual voting helps make Hashgraph quicker and more secure than blockchain according to Swirlds.

Graphchain

Another distributed consensus technology is **graphchain**. The significant difference between blockchain and graphchain is that graphchain does not store blocks or transaction information. Information is stored in the nodes or edges of the graphchain.

[N]odes are identified by a public key and its information is controlled by the corresponding private key holder. Edges represent relationships between the entities controlling nodes and some of these relationships can only be added to the graphchain if they are signed by the private keys of both connected nodes. [xlii]

The nodes determine the type and conditions of the relationship that affects edges and the information the edges contain. The purpose of the graphchain is to create an "Internet of People" in which individuals and organizations can directly contact each other and discover – with the node owner's permission – information about the node owner.

A possible application, **the Fermat Project,** is to create an "open social graph" and to support "device-to-device communication" so people can be directly accessed anywhere on the Internet of People.

The Cicada Platform

The Cicada Platform is not a technology, but a combination of distributed consensus technologies to establish a "representativeless" direct democracy. The Cicada Platform relies on two cutting-edge technologies:

A "Human Unique Identifier" (HUID) that is unique to each individual and allows complete control of the individual's personally identifying information (PII).

A variation of blockchain's "Proof of Work" miner linked to each individual. A blockchain miner performs the complex calculations to make the blockchain work. The miner in the Cicada Platform provides the distributed proof of work that makes the direct democracy portion of the Cicada Platform operate.

According to the proponents of the Cicada Platform, with these two technologies in place, all that is needed to institute a direct democracy is the Cicada Platform app running on mobile devices connected to a mesh network. "The next time there is an Arab Spring, the people will be able to replace their leaders with code."[xliii]

Does Distributed Consensus Technology Solve Democracy's Principal-Agent Problem?

A significant challenge of representational democratic government is the **principal-agent problem**. With increasing levels of distrust in government and elected representatives, could distributed consensus technologies such as the ones outlined above help solve or even eliminate the principal-agent problem of representational democracy?

LEARNING MATTERS MORE THAN RESULTS
(2017)

Even if you are not a Star Trek fan, you may have heard of the Kobayashi Maru Test. The Kobayashi Maru is a computer simulation that every Starfleet cadet faces before they can graduate. In the simulation, the cadet is the captain of a ship. During a routine patrol near enemy territory, the ship receives a distress call from a friendly ship stranded across enemy lines. The cadet can attempt to rescue the ship but risk an all-out war or leave the distressed ship's crew to certain death. If the cadet tries a rescue mission, the simulation is programmed to ensure that the rescue mission fails, and that the cadet's ship and crew are destroyed. The test is unbeatable (however, there have been a few notable exceptions).

The reason for the test is to determine how the cadet faces a no-win situation. It is a test of character in which the results don't matter as much as how the cadet made the decisions that led to their actions.

Government workers can also face variants of no-win situations in their work in which the system seems programmed to ensure failure no matter the employee's best efforts. Or circumstances and plain luck were not in the employee's favor. Either way, managers must consider which is more important to reward: the results or the employee's behavior?

Vadim Liberman writes about the two different types of jobs in the modern workplace. Algorithmic jobs are "usually lower down in an enterprise, often involve repetitive work, and feature obvious causation between input and output. Recognizing algorithmic employees for their results makes sense."

The other type of job is heuristic jobs. Heuristic jobs "demand creativity and experimentation and include tons of variables that complicate drawing clear lines between cause and effect. The line between results and recognition is consequently just as squiggly. So why draw it at all?"

People who perform heuristic jobs must feel safe to experiment and to face the occasional failure as they attempt something new and risky. Continuing to reward and punish based on results will teach people to become risk-averse and timid.

I can already anticipate the first objection; if people are not rewarded for results, then they will not try as hard to achieve results. The solution to that issue is to instill a growth mindset in your employees so they see failure as a learning experience and will work harder next time to achieve a better result.

When employees have the mindset that it is their hard work that makes them more successful and smarter about their work, they will be intrinsically motivated to do better. Rewarding behaviors that encourage learning and self-development will better ensure good results because the organization is essentially supporting the employees to create their own "good luck."

Another problem with rewarding people solely for the results they produce is that it is a false dichotomy. One is successful or fails. However, is a success or failure really what they seem? For example, is Google a successful company?

Google succeeds because it has had many failures that helped it learn and grow its successes. Is the Sydney Opera House a success or failure? It cost much more than initially planned and took much longer to build than anticipated. It was considered a failed project at the time but now is the most iconic building in the world.

In a volatile, uncertain, complex, and ambiguous (VUAC) world, success and failure are not as fixed as one would believe. The real key to success in the VUAC world is people and organizations that can quickly learn and adapt to rapid change Rewarding people for how much they have learned and grown will produce more desired results rather than just rewarding for good results alone.

(Originally appeared in *GovLoop*)

COST-BENEFIT ANALYSIS OR COST-VALUE ANALYSIS? (2018)

The Sydney Opera House is my favorite example when discussing what makes a project successful. Construction started in 1957 with a projected budget of seven million dollars. The Sydney Opera House was expected to be completed in 1963 but was completed in 1973 and over 94 million dollars in costs. Jorn Utzon, the original architect, resigned from the project in 1966 after severe criticism from the Australian government.

So great was the animosity between Utzon and the Australian government that his name was not mentioned during the formal opening on October 20, 1973. Massively over-budget and way behind schedule, the Sydney Opera House should be considered a major project failure.

However, Utzon won the highest honor in architecture (the Prizker Architecture Prize) in 2003 because of his design for the Sydney Opera House. The Sydney Opera House is beloved by the Australian people and, in 2007, became a UNESCO World Heritage Site. In its 45-year history, the Sydney Opera House has more than made up for its budget overruns and delayed opening.

By a strict cost-benefit analysis performed on the opening of the Opera House, the project would have been considered a failure. Yet, the Sydney Opera House has evolved into a resounding success with great value to the Australian people.

Cass R. Sunstein's The Cost-Benefit Revolution

Mr. Sunstein recently published his argument for using cost-benefit analysis in deciding public policy issues. Now a professor at Harvard, Mr. Sunstein was the Administrator of the White House Office of Information and Regulatory Affairs (OIRA) in the President Obama administration. As the OIRA Administrator, Sunstein reviewed all proposed federal regulation to determine if the benefits of the regulation outweigh the costs of the regulation.

He speaks about his experiences at the OIRA office and how the cost-benefit approach was established under President Reagan. Sunstein argues that *expressivism* is responsible for the inability to resolve public policy issues.

Expressivism versus Cost-Benefit Analysis

Sunstein defines expressivism as people focusing on the values inherent in the public policy issue. He argues that focusing on values causes unnecessary conflict and that the solution is to focus on the facts of a public policy issue.

Cost-benefit analysis requires a real need for government intervention because of market failure and that the best people to intervene are the experts in the particular regulatory domain. Using cost-benefit analysis will increase welfare while respecting individual autonomy.

A key concept in using cost-benefit analysis for public policy is the *value of a statistical life* (VSL). According to Sunstein, the value of human life is around nine million dollars. All regulations will involve the tradeoff between the cost of preserving life versus a loss of autonomy implied by the regulation. "If we want to be precise, the government is assessing the *value of reducing statistical risks of death* [italics in original]," writes Sunstein.

The rest of his book explores the ramifications of his VSL approach to regulation. In his conclusion, Sunstein argues that the "cost-benefit revolution has produced immeasurable improvements. It has stopped bad things, spurred good things, and turned good things into better things." However, he gives the caveat that cost-benefit analysis works when the study is done correctly, and public officials followed the recommendations of the cost-benefit analysis.

Benefits Versus Value

Sunstein's book argues for using cost-benefit analysis in justifying the need for some government regulations. Claiming that ALL government regulations should be justified by cost-benefit analysis conflicts with the values of the U.S. Constitution and democratic ideals. Sunstein, early in his book, assumes that regulation is only necessary to compensate for market failure.

In Part II of the book, Sunstein considers how to apply cost-benefit analysis to values such as privacy or freedom of speech. Again, the decision still reduces the cost of preserving the value versus the VSL. Sunstein is right that focusing only on the values in public policy can lead to indecision or bad decisions. Where Sunstein errs is the overreliance on the benefits of a proposed public policy.

What is needed is a balance between benefits and value. The reason is that it is difficult to predict the eventual benefits and values of public policy or regulation. As with the Sydney Opera House example, a public project could start as a tremendous failure. Over time, this same failure could emerge as a success. Or, a public project, such as the Apollo Moon landings could be considered not worth the costs because the direct benefits are not enough to justify the immediate costs.

However, the indirect benefits such as the technological innovations of computer miniaturization and advanced manufacturing technologies. Costs can be immediately quantified and calculated. In the project management world, costing methods are mature and robust.

Determining the benefits of a project is still evolving as reflected in the discipline of *benefits realization management*.[xliv] What is missing in Sunstein's cost-benefit analysis is the time element. Without sufficient time for benefits to appear, the value of public regulation or project can be erroneously assessed.

WHY THE OFFICE OF TECHNOLOGY ASSESSMENT IS NEEDED NOW MORE THAN EVER (2019)

We've arranged a global civilization in which most crucial elements profoundly depend on science and technology. We have also arranged things so that almost no one understands science and technology. This is a prescription for disaster. We might get away with it for a while, but sooner or later this combustible mixture of ignorance and power is going to blow up in our faces.

— Carl Sagan, *The Demon-Haunted World: Science as a Candle in the Dark*

The *Washington Post* Editorial Board published an editorial on September 17, 2018, in which they, again, argued for the restoration of the Office of Technology Assessment. After observing how federal legislators struggled with questioning Facebook, Google, Amazon, and other large technology companies, the Editorial Board wrote that it is "**crucial for legislators to grapple with technological issues on a higher level than most have so far proved themselves capable.**"

Before its defunding in 1995, the Office of Technology Assessment (OTA) provided Congress with nonpartisan science and technology analysis. Created in 1972, the OTA produced over 750 studies on issues about acid rain, climate change, supersonic transports, and even health care.

The OTA was an early pioneer in electronic publishing, and other governments copied the OTA model. It is an irony that the OTA was defunded the year that the commercial Internet played an increasing role in the American economy and culture.

Social Technologies and Mind Hacking

During a recent flight to an academic conference, I read Roger McNamee's *Zucked: Waking Up to the Facebook Catastrophe* (2019). McNamee was a mentor and angel investor in Facebook before he became increasingly concerned about the psychological effects of Facebook on its users. McNamee describes how Facebook's management used the platform to push users to act impulsively and aided the rise of fake news - "brain hacking."

The purpose of this brain hacking is to create more effective platforms for advertising. But the effort is wasted if we retain our ability to resist it. Circumventing the ability to resist brain hacking is why Facebook (according to a leaked report Facebook sent to an advertiser) developed tools to determine when teenagers using its network feel insecure, worthless or stressed. These appear to be the optimum moments for hitting them with a micro-targeted promotion. Facebook denies that it offered "tools to target people based on their emotional state."[xlv]

The Congressional hearings into Facebook's practices were to expose the widespread use of brain hacking and the problems of fake news. However, as anyone who watched the hearings could observe, Congressional members could barely ask even basic questions about social networking technologies.

I argue that if OTA was still in existence, the Congress could be doing a better job in understanding and mitigating the harmful effects of social technologies on consumers and the American political process.

The Effect of Automation on America's Labor Market

Another issue that needs a nonpartisan analysis is the effect of automation on the U.S. workforce. One set of studies shows there will be widespread displacement leading to millions out of work while other studies argue for significant benefits to the U.S. worker.[xlvi]

Again, the OTA would be useful in helping legislators cut through all the noise and determine what the most probable scenarios for the economy are. The OTA studies could help Congress get in front of the automation issue to draft legislation that will increase the benefits of automation while preventing downsides of a newly-displaced workforce.

OTA's studies could also guide education policy as universities, colleges, and K-12 schools determine how to best prepare children today for the jobs of tomorrow. There are many scattered STEM initiatives across the country that address different aspects of preparing students for STEM careers. Helpful is a series of reports from a newly-resurrected OTA that can inform Congress' education legislation.

Climate Change, Interrupted

Although never proven but suspected, is the motive behind the defunding of the OTA. According to some observers, the OTA reports on health care reform, environmental issues, and the dangers of technologies such as nuclear power lead to widespread resistance by businesses and interest groups with a stake in preventing further regulation. Probably the most controversial OTA studies were centered on the dangers of climate change.

Given the dangers posed by climate change almost 25 years after the defunding of OTA, it is understandable why some legislators have continually introduced legislation to reestablish the OTA. Technology is playing an even more significant role in the American economy and society as well as posing potential threats to our national security. Now, more than ever, Congress needs a non-partisan and informed voice to help legislators confront and manage the dangers of our highly-technological world.

Gov Trek

In my online University of Louisville class on communication technology, we discuss the history of communication technology from the days of cave paintings to the latest in virtual and augmented reality. As the coda to the course, we examine four possible future worlds created by the new digital technologies.

The first two worlds come classic dystopian literature. Either the new digital technologies create a *1984*-style future of constant surveillance in an authoritarian state, or we amuse ourselves to death in a *Brave New World* future. Some students remarked that we have seemed to have achieved a *Brave New 1984* world where our constant surveillance technologies can also amuse us as the AIs observe us ("Alexa, can cats eat pancakes?").

The third world is influenced by my first viewing of *Terminator*. As our digital technologies become smarter, will there be a time when the machines replace us? Maybe not to the extent that the AI superintelligences will attempt to exterminate humanity. However, there are real concerns in the public and private sectors of how many people will lose jobs to the increasing automation of work. The students have a great time discussing a post-work world but, I can sense the underlying fear they have in wondering if their college education will be worth anything in the post-work world.

The fourth world is the optimistic future created by Gene Roddenberry's *Star Trek*. *Star Trek* has been a significant influence on my life having grown up in the 70s with constant reruns of the original series. In the *Star Trek* world, humanity has adapted to a post-scarcity world abundant with amazing technologies such as antigravity, transporters, replicators, and warp drive. Public administration, in the form of the Federation, is an honored and valuable part of life as the Federation's citizens face numerous threats from the Borg to Romulans to the occasional renegade Starfleet officer.

I think you can see hints of the four worlds in my essays. Whether it is the concern around social technologies and how social technologies have seemed to create the *Brave New 1984*. Or how federal government workers can thrive in the new workplace automation world. I also see how the federal government along with the state and local governments seem to move toward the GovTrek world.

So, where do I see the federal, state, and local governments in terms of the original four scenarios? Again, there is a mix but, I feel optimistic in that all governments seem to be moving toward InnoGov in terms of Philip K. Dick's observation that the future has arrived. It's just that InnoGov is not equally distributed – yet.

Still there are parts of government stuck in SteamGov such as the short time I worked at the U.S. Department of Agriculture. As the manager of the Human Resources Information Management Branch, I struggled weekly to pull HR reports from a Cobol mainframe that contained the payroll and personnel information for a quarter of the federal civilian workforce.

Then, there is GoogleGov which should be renamed "PublicPrivateGov" as public-private partnership proliferated in the last decade. As more public agencies move to the cloud, companies like Google and Amazon have benefited from hosting the agency functions of federal, state, and local governments. In the state and local government sector, numerous govtech companies have sprung up while the open source revolution has become an essential part of the federal government.

LabGov is alive and well in the state and local governments. Each issue of *Governing, Government Technology* and related magazines on state and local government showcases the latest state and local technology and policy innovations. There are many lessons that state and local governments can teach the federal government on how to best use digital technologies.

Finally, there are pockets of InnoGov in the federal government. For several years, I chronicled the latest innovations in my DigitalGov *Data Briefing* column. As I have expressed in the essays, it is more a cultural barrier than a technology barrier holding InnoGov back.

I think that the federal, state, and local governments are on the path to Gov Trek. As any *Star Trek* fan will tell you, the road to the Federation was difficult. There were many stops and starts, detours and dead ends, and opposition both internal and external to realizing the vision and ideals of the Federation. I hope that my essays chronical some part of the journey for the federal, state, and local governments in this new century.

ABOUT THE AUTHOR

You read most of my biography in the Introduction so, no need to recap here. I love hearing from readers, and I invite you to connect with me on LinkedIn at https://www.linkedin.com/in/billbrantley/. Comment on my column and the other great columnists at *PA Times* (https://patimes.org/). Check out my personal blog at BillBrantley.com where I talk about public administration, project management, communication, and sometimes, about cats.

If you liked this book, please leave a review on Amazon. Or if you didn't like this book, still leave a review. I especially like talking to folks who disagree with me. Keeps me honest.

Also, if you are a project manager or want to learn more about business communication, please check out my other book, *The Persuasive Project Manager* (https://www.amazon.com/dp/B07NCC7KFN) on Amazon.com.

Endnotes

[i] http://www.imdb.com/title/tt0052077/

[ii] https://opengovdirective.pbworks.com/w/page/NASA-OpenGov-Community-Summit

[iii]

http://money.cnn.com/magazines/business2/business2_archive/2006/01/01/8368125/index.htm

[iv] http://en.wikipedia.org/wiki/Steam_punk

[v] http://www.govtrack.us/congress/bill.xpd?bill=h111-5238

[vi] read the original 1972 paper at http://www.unc.edu/~fbaum/teaching/articles/Cohen_March_Olsen_1972.pdf

[vii] report found at http://www.gao.gov/products/GAO-16-696T

[viii] https://www.networksasia.net/article/early-blockchain-success-will-be-limited-gartner.1502766720

[ix] https://fcw.com/articles/2018/03/20/trump-management-agenda.aspx

[x] https://irpaai.com/definition-and-benefits/

[xi] http://www.governing.com/topics/mgmt/gov-reinventing-government-book.html

[xii] http://info.profilesinternational.com/profiles-employee-assessment-blog/bid/208850/Increase-Employee-Engagement-by-Developing-Employee-Skills

xiii http://www.lindseypollak.com/how-training-and-development-opportunities-boost-millennials-employee-satisfaction/

xiv https://www.linkedin.com/pulse/corporate-talent-management-dead-josh-bersin

xv http://www.pmi.org/-/media/pmi/documents/public/pdf/business-solutions/improve-program-management-federal-government.pdf

xvi http://www.governing.com/columns/smart-mgmt/col-how-academia-failing-government.html

xvii http://www.governing.com/columns/smart-mgmt/col-what-public-administration-schools-could-do-for-government.html

xviii https://www.amazon.com/Gen-Work-Generation-Transforming-Workplace-ebook/dp/B01HM27IDK/ref=tmm_kin_swatch_0?_encoding=UTF8&qid=1497730182&sr=8-1-fkmr0

xix http://www.washingtonpost.com/sf/style/2016/05/25/inside-the-race-to-decipher-todays-teens-who-will-transform-society-as-we-know-it/?utm_term=.21ce5663d800

xx https://dupress.deloitte.com/dup-us-en/focus/human-capital-trends/2017/future-workforce-changing-nature-of-work.html

xxi http://www.zdnet.com/article/robots-will-replace-250000-government-jobs-and-thats-just-the-beginning/

xxii http://patimes.org/government-leadership-gap-leads-employee-engagement/

xxiii Dinh, J.E., Lord, R.G., Gardner, W.L., Meuser, J.D., Liden, R.C., & Hu, J. (2014). Leadership theory and research in the new millennium: Current theoretical trends and changing perspectives. *The Leadership Quarterly, 25*(1), 36-62

xxiv https://www.forbes.com/sites/parmyolson/2018/02/15/the-algorithm-that-helped-google-translate-become-sexist/#1cdee95e7daa

xxv https://www.forbes.com/sites/parmyolson/2018/02/15/the-algorithm-that-helped-google-translate-become-sexist/#1cdee95e7daa

xxvi https://www.govexec.com/excellence/management-matters/2018/12/improving-program-management/153825/?oref=govexec_today_pm_nl

xxvii

http://businessofgovernment.org/sites/default/files/A%20Framework%20for%20Improving%20Federal%20Program%20Management_1.pdf

xxviii https://www.pmi.org/learning/thought-leadership/series/benefits-realization/strengthening-benefits-awareness-csuite-eiu

xxix http://www.six-sig.com/index.php/lss-news/19-500-million-stakeholders

xxx http://www.informationweek.com/software/information-management/government-as-a-platform-not-a-vending-machine/d/d-id/1082242?

xxxi

http://www.sciencedirect.com/science/article/pii/S0740624X1630003X

xxxii http://www.fas.org/sgp/crs/misc/R44331.pdf

xxxiii

https://www.whitehouse.gov/blog/2016/10/12/administrations-report-future-artificial-intelligence

xxxiv https://www.whitehouse.gov/blog/2016/12/20/artificial-intelligence-automation-and-economy

xxxv http://www.pewresearch.org/fact-tank/2018/04/26/key-findings-on-americans-views-of-the-u-s-political-system-and-democracy/

xxxvi

https://www.theatlantic.com/business/archive/2017/10/graham-cassidy-states-federal-efficiency/541599/

xxxvii https://link.springer.com/article/10.1007/s11077-018-9321-9

xxxviii

https://www.tandfonline.com/doi/abs/10.1080/10570318209374077

xxxix

https://www.jstor.org/stable/20159074?seq=1#page_scan_tab_contents

xl https://ac.els-cdn.com/S1877042813027869/1-s2.0-S1877042813027869-main.pdf?_tid=5a572d49-685c-424c-b5dc-bf0bb2cb7d7f&acdnat=1534077977_a4565c9f3d21261c44d215e11efe8f2e

xli http://www.scientificamerican.com/article.cfm?id=the-economist-has-no-clothes

xlii https://hackernoon.com/introducing-the-graphchain-2d20513bf713

xliii https://github.com/the-laughing-monkey/cicada-platform

xliv https://www.pmi.org/-
/media/pmi/documents/public/pdf/learning/thought-
leadership/benefits-realization-management-framework.pdf

xlv https://www.monbiot.com/2019/01/06/the-mind-hackers/

xlvi https://www.mckinsey.com/mgi/overview/in-the-
news/automation-and-the-future-of-work

www.ingramcontent.com/pod-product-compliance
Lightning Source LLC
Chambersburg PA
CBHW051346280526
45784CB00007B/2836